Essential Guides for
EARLY CAREER TEACHERS

Assessment

Essential Guides for Early Career Teachers

The *Essential Guides for Early Career Teachers* provide accessible, carefully researched, quick-reads for early career teachers, covering the key topics you will encounter during your training year and first two years of teaching. They complement and are fully in line with the new Early Career Framework and are intended to assist on-going professional development by bringing together current information and thinking on each area in one convenient place. The texts are edited by Emma Hollis, Executive Director of NASBTT (the National Association of School-Based Teacher Trainers), who brings a wealth of experience, expertise and knowledge to the series.

There are three books in the series so far but look out for more as the series develops.

Essential Guides for Early Career Teachers: Assessment
Alys Finch
Paperback ISBN: 978-1-912508-93-8

Essential Guides for Early Career Teachers: Mental Well-being and Self Care
Sally Price
Paperback ISBN: 978-1-912508-97-6

Essential Guides for Early Career Teachers: Special Educational Needs and Disability
Anita Devi
Paperback ISBN: 978-1-913063-29-0

Our titles are also available in a range of electronic formats. To order, or for details of our bulk discounts, please go to our website www.criticalpublishing.com or contact our distributor, NBN International, 10 Thornbury Road, Plymouth PL6 7PP, telephone 01752 202301 or email orders@nbninternational.com.

Essential Guides for
EARLY CAREER
TEACHERS

Assessment

Alys Finch
Series editor: Emma Hollis

First published in 2019 by Critical Publishing Ltd

British Library Cataloguing in Publication Data
A CIP record for this book is available from the British Library

ISBN: 978-1-912508-93-8

This book is also available in the following e-book formats:

MOBI ISBN: 978-1-912508-94-5
EPUB ISBN: 978-1-912508-95-2
Adobe e-book ISBN: 978-1-912508-96-9

Cartoon illustrations by Élisabeth Eudes-Pascal represented by GCI
Cover and text design by Out of House Limited
Project Management by Newgen Publishing UK
Printed and bound in Great Britain by 4edge, Essex

Critical Publishing
3 Connaught Road
St Albans
AL3 5RX

www.criticalpublishing.com

Paper from responsible sources

Contents

Meet the series editor

Emma Hollis

I am Executive Director of NASBTT (the National Association of School-Based Teacher Trainers) and my absolute passion is teacher education. After gaining a first-class degree in psychology I trained as a primary teacher, and soon became head of Initial Teacher Training for a SCITT provider. I am dedicated to ensuring teachers are given access to high-quality professional development at the early stages of and throughout their careers.

Meet the author

Alys Finch

I am the senior education lead for an educational trust in the Midlands. Prior to that, I was an education consultant, predominantly working with school-based teacher training providers to support excellent training for teachers and their mentors to maximise their impact on pupils. Drawing on over 15 years of teaching experience, including leading on curriculum, assessment and training at middle and senior leader levels (in schools, and in a range of local and national Initial Teacher Training contexts), I know that practical but critically engaged approaches to assessment lie at the heart of enabling and accelerating all learners' progress. Perhaps as a coffee-break read or as part of your staff/CPD meetings, I hope that a brief exploration of the ideas and approaches in this book will provide some practical ways forward for you and your pupils. You can dip and in out of this book: see where ten minutes of reading can take you – and your students!

Foreword

As a passionate advocate of high-quality teacher education and continuing professional development, it has always been a source of frustration for me that beyond the ITT year, access to high-quality, structured ongoing professional development has been something of a lottery for teachers. Access and support have been patchy, with some schools and local authorities offering fantastic opportunities for teachers throughout their careers, while in other locations CPD has been given lip service at best and, at worst, is non-existent.

This series was conceived to attempt to close some of these gaps and to offer accessible professional learning to busy teachers in the early stages of their careers. It was therefore a moment of genuine pleasure when proposals for an entitlement for all early career teachers to receive a package of support, guidance and education landed on my desk. There is now a real opportunity for school communities to work together to offer the very best early career development for our most precious of resources – the teachers in our schools.

The aim of this series is to distil some of the key topics which occupy the thoughts of early career teachers into digestible, informative texts which promote discussion, contemplation and reflection and will spark further exploration into practice. In each edition, you will find a series of practical suggestions for how you can put the 'big idea' in each chapter into practice – now, next week and in the long term. By offering opportunities to bring the learning into the classroom in a very concrete way, we hope to help embed many of the principles that are shared into day-to-day teaching.

In this first book in the series, Alys Finch explores a complex yet vital aspect of teaching: assessment. Her book makes manageable a topic which has often been fraught with confusion, myth and frustration and brings it to life in a pragmatic, practical and accessible way. Drawing on relevant research and practical experience, Alys guides the reader through some of the key principles and ideas behind assessment and offers ways in which to apply these to everyday practice.

I hope you enjoy exploring this book as much as I have enjoyed editing it.

Emma Hollis
Executive Director, NASBTT

Introduction

'Assessment' is a core aspect of all that we do in education: assessing others, assessing ourselves, assessing the impact of our work. It's a broad term which houses a wide range of processes, purposes, politics and pedagogies: negotiating the world of assessment can seem complex at best and impossibly confusing at worst.

This book aims to give you a path through the myriad facets of what can be meant by 'assessment' and some starting points for your own negotiation of this world to enable you to both maximise the positive impact of assessment on your learners and to begin to forge your own understanding of it. It should provoke as many questions as it answers: you'll leave its pages with a sense of your learning about assessment rather than with all that you ever need to know. It is intended to look at core ideas, key questions and to support you in your own construction of a definition of what 'assessment' means.

For the purposes of this book, the following definitions are used as a starting point for discussions, tasks and suggestions for further reading. They are based on the ideas and thinking outlined in this chapter. As you will see from the discussion which follows, there are ways in which the activities/strategies/approaches/interventions used for each of these aspects of assessment might overlap: the nuance between them is largely due to the intention of the use of that approach, in terms of future implications for both a teacher's practice and the learner's progress. There is a further discussion of some key terms and definitions for the purposes of this book in Chapter 1, 'The story so far'.

>> **Assessment for learning (AfL)** – activities/strategies/approaches/interventions used to support, challenge and extend learning. These might include: targeted questioning; confidence checks; checks on key skills; 'live marking'; revision activities; plenaries. Feedback is used to both check and build on learning by using the assessment as a key learning tool. The feedback is usually formative (ie developmental and focused on enabling progress rather than an end outcome) and intended to support the learner in their learning.

>> **Assessment of learning (AoL)** – activities/strategies/approaches/interventions used to check on what learning has taken place. This might include: end-of-unit tests; written exercises; presentations. Often done through outcomes-based tasks, the feedback is usually summative (ie one marker in time) and intended to check on where a learner has arrived at in their learning.

» Assessment for planning (AfP) – this is closely related to AfL in that assessments of learners are used to inform, shape and adapt future planning. This could include: using the misconceptions revealed in a task in one lesson to inform the focus of the next lesson, in which addressing these misconceptions now becomes the priority.

Assessment will be a part of your everyday work as a teacher. Hopefully, this book will enable you to begin to construct your own framework for developing the depth and breadth of your professional knowledge, as well as providing opportunities to think practically about what you do on a daily, termly, yearly and career-long basis. Indeed, it is intended to be a chance for you to *do* assessment for learning.

Chapter 1   The story so far

What? (The big idea)

A brief history of assessment

This chapter presents a brief history of assessment in schools. The intention is to give you the 'story so far' in terms of what might be meant by the broad term 'assessment', an outline of some of the key thinking about assessment over the past 30 years and some initial ways in which you might think about your own practice against this 'big picture' backdrop.

Let's travel back to the late 1980s to start a timeline of the development of conceptions and forms of assessment. There are key moments since then that are explored as we come to the more recent past (2010 to present) and where thinking about assessment currently falls. Of course, 'assessment' has been around for as long as there have been learners, but this timeframe is a manageable starting point for you as an early career teacher to contextualise your practice and that of the settings in which you are working.

Throughout this period

National curriculum, associated tests, GCSEs and the rest...

In England and Wales, the specifications published by examination boards have heavily influenced the forms of summative assessments used in Key Stages 4 and 5 (16–19 years of age). Some of the qualifications offered in these key stages include: GCSEs; Business and Technology Education Council Awards (BTECs); Advanced Subsidiary and Advanced Levels (AS and A levels); and General National Vocational Qualifications (GNVQs).

Late 1980s

National curriculum

The national curriculum was introduced in 1988 through the Education Reform Act for teaching from September 1989. This 'new' curriculum was intended to ensure parity of educational experience for pupils in state schools across England and Wales. In subsequent years, instructions for education in Wales have devolved to the Welsh government, in line with a number of other government-led systems.

The current national curriculum in England was published in 2014 (with some aspects of this statutory document introduced the following year). It focuses on education for 5–16 year-olds, linking to Key Stages (1, 2, 3 and 4) as grouped by age range (Key Stage 1, ages 5–7 years; Key Stage 2, ages 7–11 years; Key Stage 3, ages 11–14 years; Key Stage 4, ages 14–16 years). For each of the key stages, there is a statutory list of prescribed subjects: for each of these, the Secretary of State for Education provides a 'programme of study'. Each of these programmes of study sets out the content, ideas, skills and concepts to be taught for the given subject area in that key stage.

In this 'national curriculum', levels of attainment were both aligned with General Certificate of Secondary Education (GCSE) grades and linked to age phases (what are now referred to as the key stages in England and Wales).

Initially, the key mode of assessment associated with the national curriculum were GCSEs. As the national curriculum became established in the early 1990s, additional modes of testing and assessing were introduced (see below).

Assessment Reform Group

This volunteer group of researchers was brought together in 1989 and was initially known as the Policy Task Group for Assessment, then the Assessment Reform Group and latterly as the ARG (the group was dissolved in 2010). The group was convened by the British Educational Research Association (BERA – their support of such groups ended in 1996). The aim of the group was to ensure that appropriate research evidence informed educational policies and practices at all levels of the sector and government.

1990s

Standardised Attainment Tests (SATs)

Standardised Attainment Tests (SATs) were introduced in England and Wales between 1991 and 1995. These were intended to assess pupils' attainment against the newly introduced national curriculum. These SATs took place at ages 7 (end of Key Stage 1), 11 (end of Key Stage 2) and 14 (end of Key Stage 3). SATs were focused on English, mathematics and science, seen as the 'core' subjects.

Key Stage 1 SATs came first, testing the first Key Stage 1 cohort to 'complete' the national curriculum for that key stage. At their inception, Key Stage 1 SATs were designed to be a series of tasks delivered in the classroom. It quickly became apparent that the complexity of this system might need a more formalised approach, hence the 'standardised' part of the name. The SATs for Key Stages 2 and 3 were based on more formal, externally marked and internally administered tests which were akin to the style of examinations used for the end of Key Stage 4 public examinations.

Key Stage 3 tests included an element of teacher-made assessment of pupils' attainment. For this aspect of the assessment, teachers made judgements of their pupils' attainment according to nationally published criteria. These assessments were reported alongside the externally marked examinations to provide assessment outcome data for schools and parents (and, later, league tables – see below).

SATs for all three of the key stages assessed using them were graded according to a nationally published scale of 'levels'. These levels were numbered 1 to 8, with 1 being the lowest level of attainment and 8 the highest (there was also the possibility of 'exceptional performance' or 'EP' for those pupils operating above level 8 at Key Stage 3). There was a nationally set expectation of pupils' attainment for each key stage: level 2 for the end of Key Stage 1; level 4 for the end of Key Stage 2; level 5 or 6 for the end of Key Stage 3.

League tables

League tables, based on summaries of the average attainment performance of pupils, were first published in England in 1992. The focus of these league tables was to rank schools according to the GCSE performances of their pupils. League tables are published annually and link with key accountability measures for schools as set out by the Department for Education.

The Dearing Review

Published in 1996 but commissioned in 1993, Ron Dearing's review of the national curriculum was intended to look at ways of ensuring and developing the rigour of the qualifications framework for post-16 students.

Dearing's recommendations included that:

>> there should be a national framework of qualifications, encompassing 'academic' and 'vocational' qualifications;

>> awarding bodies should work more closely together;

>> the qualifications framework should be clearer about the purpose and skills for focus in qualifications;

>> consistency in standards across A levels was needed;

>> a reframed 'Advanced Subsidiary' level should be in place (AS levels);

>> qualifications should recognise a wider range of 'achievement';

>> the analysis of candidates' achievements should include wider data sub-sets, including (but not exclusively): gender, socioeconomic group and identified educational needs.

These recommendations led to some qualification reform and influenced the kinds of data analysed (from teachers to government) to interrogate pupil performance.

Black and Wiliam's 'black box'

Inside the Black Box was published in 1998. It is widely considered to be a cornerstone of the thinking which placed formative modes of assessment at the heart of the discussion. This focus on formative assessment has remained central to what we consider to be 'assessment for learning': Black and Wiliam's work from 1998 and since has led the debate about practices and pedadogy associated with assessment at all levels. This work was funded by the Assessment Reform Group (of which they were both members).

The work, undertaken between 1996 and 1998, was a literature review which sought to explore assessment used to support learning. In their findings, Black and Wiliam shared persuasive evidence that assessment could be used to improve learning when used in a 'formative' way. That is to say that assessment could be a developmental tool for learners instead of (or as well as) simply to check on what learning had taken place.

Inside the Black Box (1998) was aimed at practitioners and was the publication which resulted from the ARG-funded work.

The Assessment Reform Group used further funding to extend the ideas, examples and practices of *Inside the Black Box* in their 1999 publication, *Assessment for Learning: Beyond the Black Box*. Black and Wiliam were also in the team behind this publication.

2000s

SATs

From 2005, Key Stage 1 SATs were no longer used in external data. Instead, they were used internally in schools to support teachers' judgements of pupils' attainment.

2008 saw the end of Key Stage 3 SATs. No formal, externally reported assessments were created to replace them.

League tables

Information used for various published league tables during this period included: SATs performances for primary and secondary schools; GCSE performances for secondary schools (Goldstein and Leckie, 2016).

Responses to Black and Wiliam

The 2000s saw a prolific response to Black and Wiliam's work. In the first instance, promoted by the Assessment Reform Group's 1999 response to, and extension of, *Inside the Black Box*, this was seen in an explosion of teachers 'doing AfL'.

The Assessment Reform Group took the opportunity to take the research-informed discussion a further step forward. In 2002, the group (comprising Black, Harrison, Lee, Marshall and Wiliam) published advice for teachers to improve their classroom practice using formative assessment principles (*Working Inside the Black Box*, 2002). This programme, which included close work with teachers, sought to make practical the pedagogy from the 'black boxes' of 1998 and 1999.

Indeed, Black and Wiliam published work taking the ideas of their 1998 publication further. Their 2006 chapter, 'Assessment for Learning in the Classroom' in *Assessment and Learning* (ed. Gardner, 2006), laid out practical approaches to embedding the full depth of the principles that they had espoused in their earlier work. This was an attempt to clarify and 'make real' the ideas of *Inside the Black Box*, seeking to ensure reflective, theoretical depth to the increasingly lively and plentiful discussions of 'doing AfL' emerging during this period.

In recognition of the explicit focus now seeming to be placed on AfL and its potential power, and to investigate the efficacy of emerging practices, the (then titled) Department for Children, Schools and Families (DCSF) launched 'Making Good Progress' in 2007. This pilot included: developing resources for 'assessing pupils' progress'; an overt focus on AfL; tests; tuition for individual pupils; and a premium for pupil progression. Ofsted authored the report which looked at the impact of this pilot project. It focused on the project's impact on improving pupils' outcomes (attainment and achievement) and the efficacy of the approaches in ensuring that pupils' needs were met and learning was supported. The study, published in 2011 (findings for the report were finalised in 2010), found that the impact of the project was greatest when assessment was seen as an integral part of teaching and learning, led at a whole-school level. The report commented that athough it was impossible to pinpoint the exact impact of the project as the schools seen mostly used it as part of a range of assessment foci, the pilot did universally improve assessment practices in the schools in the sample.

2010s – the present

Life without levels

In 2010 an expert panel convened by the then Secretary of State for Education, Michael Gove, recommended the abolition of levels.

Dylan Wiliam was part of this panel: his input to the group was a clear desire to move to non-age-indexed levels. These levels would recognise the idea of a continuum of proficiency. Wiliam's model was intended to suggest that 'progress' along this continuum might be possible for *all* pupils and, therefore, the levels would be motivational (Wiliam cited in Christodoulou, 2017, p 7).

The Commission on Assessment Without Levels was set up in February 2015 by the then Secretary of State for Education, Nicky Morgan, to further explore the implications of removing levels. At the centre of its rationale, the Commission stated that:

Despite being intended only for use in statutory national assessments, too frequently levels also came to be used for in-school assessment between key stages in order to monitor whether pupils were on track to achieve expected levels at the end of key stages. This distorted the purpose of in-school assessment, particularly day-to-day formative assessment. The Commission believes that this has had a profoundly negative impact on teaching.

Too often levels became viewed as thresholds and teaching became focused on getting pupils across the next threshold instead of ensuring they were secure in the knowledge and understanding defined in the programmes of study. Depth and breadth of understanding were sometimes sacrificed in favour of pace. Levels also used a 'best fit' model, which meant that a pupil could have serious gaps in their knowledge and understanding, but still be placed within the level. This meant it wasn't always clear exactly which areas of the curriculum the child was secure in and where the gaps were.

(DfE, 2015, p 5)

Attempting to redress the balance that the Commission felt was lacking in assessment practices in schools, their recommendations included suggesting that assessment be in the 'core curriculum' for Initial Teacher Training (programmes leading to the award of Qualified Teacher Status). This was a further development of the commentary in the report which felt that the establishment of commonly understood assessment principles should be key to schools' assessment policies. The Commission's *Final Report of the Commission on Assessment Without Levels* was published in September 2015.

Tests in primary schools

2016 saw the end of SATs from the old model. Assessments for Key Stages 1 and 2 are now a combination of tests and teacher assessments which result in a judgement about a child's attainment.

Linking back to the 'old SATs' used in primary schools, National Foundation for Educational Research (NFER) tests became optional for primary schools around this time.

Changes to GCSE grades

In 2017, new grades were introduced for GCSEs. There was a move from using A*–G to 9–1 for GCSE grades. Although there is no exact equivalence between the numerical and lettered grades, grades 4–6 are deemed to be roughly equivalent to grades C–B in the previous system.

League tables

League tables continue to report on schools' performance according to pupils' GCSE attainment in English (language and/or literature, or combined) and mathematics. Information in these tables reports on pupils achieving grade 5 or above (a 'strong pass') and also those achieving grade 4 or above (a 'standard pass').

There are also league tables which rank schools according to English Baccalaureate ('EBacc') attainment scores. The 'EBacc' is a suite of six 'core' GCSE subjects (as set out by the DfE) which includes: English, mathematics, combined science (counting as two subjects), history or geography and a language. Though all students must take both English language and literature, they only need a grade 5 or above (in the new grades) in one of them for it to count in their EBacc profile.

Information used for various published league tables during this period began to include 'Progress 8' scores. 'Progress 8' and 'Attainment 8' are designed to assess pupils' progress between the end of primary school (end of Key Stage 2) and the end of Key Stage 4. These measures look at pupils' attainment scores in English and mathematics (worth double in value for the score) and four other qualifications. The additional qualifications include: up to three subjects from the EBacc list; the pupil's three highest scores from a range of other qualifications (GCSEs and non-GCSEs).

A return to and a development of the ideas from *Inside the Black Box* (1998)?

Daisy Christodoulou's 2017 book, *Making Good Progress? The Future of Assessment for Learning,* could be seen as part of the change that may be possible as schools really look at what assessment could and should be doing. Christodoulou's relationship with Wiliam's ideas is profound, even in his endorsing foreword to her book. Throughout the book, the idea that progress is about how far pupils have come rather than how far they've fallen short of or surpassed a target is placed at the centre of developing an understanding of what assessment can do as part of pupils' learning.

Nikki Booth's 2017 article in the Chartered College for Teaching's journal, *Impact,* highlighted several key practices which her reading identified as being key to using assessment as a developmental learning tool: learning intentions; success criteria; eliciting (quality) evidence of pupil learning; feedback; peer- and self-assessment.

Both of these publications were indicative of two key questions threading through the debates of the 20 years between their writing and the emergence of *Inside the Black Box.*

1. What do we mean by 'assessment'?

2. How can we use assessment (in schools and in individual classrooms) to make a positive difference to pupils' learning (both in terms of outcomes and learning progression per se)?

Both of these questions were part of the impetus for Black and Wiliam's work in the 1990s and remain central to the debate about assessment at all levels of the education sector.

Working definitions derived from the 'history' of assessment

For the purposes of the discussions, tasks and questions posed in the remainder of this chapter and book as a whole, we shall assume the following definitions. These are in addition to those outlined in the introduction to this book. You will, of course, develop your own understanding of what these things mean to you, what they look like in your practice, how they are interpreted in your context and what impact they can have on your learners. Here, these definitions are intended to create a common understanding from which to develop your thinking.

>> **Assessment for Learning (AfL)** – activities/strategies/approaches/interventions used to support, challenge and extend learning (see the Introduction for more detail).

>> **Formative assessment** – assessment which takes place *during* learning; is an integral part of the learning process; highlights learners' emerging strengths; identifies learners' areas for development; provides opportunities for learners to improve.

>> **Summative assessment** – assessment which captures learners' attainment for a given outcome, often linked to descriptors of gradations of attainment pertinent to the skills, knowledge and/or attributes which have been the focus of the assessment task. These assessments can be used to generate outcomes data, such as GCSE examinations and internal end-of-unit tasks.

So what? ◀◀◀

What difference will it make?

We return to revised versions of these questions in Chapters 3, 6 and 7, where you'll have an opportunity to challenge, broaden and deepen your thinking in response to them. In this iteration of the questions/tasks, the intention is for you to think about the 'big picture' of assessment within the context of your everyday practice, your school setting and the potential impact of this on the pupils with whom you're working.

Reflective task ◀◀◀

Apply the big idea to a practical situation in the classroom

The key aim of this task is to explore how you are developing your understanding of what 'assessment' means to you as a teacher. Over time, and through the work that you'll do as part of this and other chapters in this book, you could use these 'framing' questions as a starting point for your on-going development of your professional understanding of assessment. This reflective task is a good place to start with this.

There are two broad questions underpinning this task.

1. What influences your ideas about and approaches to assessment?

2. What impact does assessment have on the children that you teach?

Reading		Feedback from colleagues		Feedback from pupils	
What have you learned?	How does this influence your practice/ thinking?	What have you learned?	How does this influence your practice/ thinking?	What have you learned?	How does this influence your practice/ thinking?
Why?	Impact on you? Impact on your pupils?	Why?	Impact on you? Impact on your pupils?	Why?	Impact on you? Impact on your pupils?

Training you've had		ASSESSMENT	Curricula/ specifications/ frameworks	
What have you learned?	How does this influence your practice/ thinking?	• What does it mean to you? • What influences your ideas about and approaches to assessment?	What have you learned?	How does this influence your practice/ thinking?
Why?	Impact on you? Impact on your pupils?	• What impact does assessment have on the children that you teach?	Why?	Impact on you? Impact on your pupils?

Tests/assessments		Observations of others		Other (anything else)	
What have you learned?	How does this influence your practice/ thinking?	What have you learned?	How does this influence your practice/ thinking?	What have you learned?	How does this influence your practice/ thinking?
Why?	Impact on you? Impact on your pupils?	Why?	Impact on you? Impact on your pupils?	Why?	Impact on you? Impact on your pupils?

Example Using the reflective task

This example looks at one of the eight areas for focus from the reflective task.

Feedback from colleagues	
What have you learned? • I tend to use assessment strategies which either look at confidence in the lesson (ie traffic light colours to show how confident the class feels after a task) or summative assessments which look at an end outcome (ie writing a comment about the quality of the work based on assessment criteria).	**How does this influence your practice/ thinking?** • I mostly plan for assessment in terms of tasks for my pupils to complete. • I mostly plan for assessment of learning. • Feedback from my colleagues' observations of my teaching has suggested that I experiment with a wider range of assessment for learning strategies.
Why? • I am focused on completing the content that needs to be delivered in a lesson. • I am keen to assess pupils' ability to complete the required tasks for the end-of-learning assessment so that I can see what they can do and what they need to improve. • I am keen to use assessment for learning to be more dynamic in using assessment to progress pupils' learning and in using information from those assessments to influence my planning.	**Impact on you?** • It has made me realise that I use a small range of strategies for similar purposes in lessons, and I mostly use assessment of learning. • An identified area for my development is to experiment with a wider range of assessment for learning strategies. **Impact on your pupils?** • Pupils can tend to focus on whether they 'got it right' rather than on what they learned. • Pupils ask about getting it right: they are reticent to ask for help in case it affects their mark for the assessment task.

Now what?

Practical ways to implement this in the classroom

Practical task for tomorrow ◀◀◀

Choose *one* lesson to focus on tomorrow. Reflect on the lesson you've chosen using the following questions to guide you.

What happened in the lesson in terms of assessment?	• • • • • •
What key questions could you ask about your practice in that lesson, based on your reflections above, that would develop your use of assessment further?	• • • • • •
What impact/experience of assessment did you want the children to have in the lesson? What actual impact/ experience was there?	• • • • • •

Why? How do you know what you know? What did this look like?	• • • • • •
What impact/experience of assessment do you want pupils to have in the next week of lessons? What might this look like?	• • • • • •

Practical task for next week ◀◀◀

Choose *three* lessons to focus on next week. Reflect on the lessons you've chosen collectively, using the following questions to guide you. The intention here is for you to build on your practice using your learning from the task above which focused on one lesson.

Key questions to use to look at how you've developed your practice, based on your reflections above.	• • • • • •

What happened in the lessons in terms of assessment? • What answers do you have to the questions that you identified from the one lesson that you looked at in the previous task (see key questions in the row above)?	• • • • • •
What key questions could you ask about your practice, based on your reflections above, that would develop your use of assessment further in the longer term?	• • • • • •
What impact/experience of assessment did you want the children to have in these lessons? What actual impact/ experience was there?	• • • • • •
Why? How do you know what you know? What did this look like?	• • • • • •

What impact/experience of assessment do you want pupils to have in the next half-term? What might this look like?	• • • • • •

Practical task for the long term ◀◀◀

Focus on these questions over the next term. Reflect on what happens in your school and in your classroom using the following questions to guide you. The intention here is for you to build on your practice using your learning from the tasks above which focused on a few lessons.

The key underpinning questions here are as follows.

• What happens in your school and in your classroom?

• What key questions might you want to ask?

• What impact/experience of assessment do you want the children that you teach to have during their time with you? Why? What might this look like?

What happens in your *school* over the term?		What happens in your *classroom* over the term?	
Key questions to use to look at how you've developed your practice based on your reflections above.	• • • • • •	Key questions to use to look at how you've developed your practice based on your reflections above.	• • • • • •
What has happened in your school in terms of the use of assessment? • What answers do you have to the questions that you identified from the lessons that you looked at in the previous tasks (see key questions in the row above)?	• • • • • • •	What happened in your classroom in terms of your use of assessment? • What answers do you have to the questions that you identified from the lessons that you looked at in the previous tasks (see key questions in the row above)?	• • • • • • •
What key questions could you ask about your practice, based on your reflections above, that would develop your use of assessment further in the next term?	• • • • • •	What key questions could you ask about your practice, based on your reflections above, that would develop your use of assessment further in the next term?	• • • • • •

What happens in your *school* over the term?		What happens in your *classroom* over the term?	
What impact/ experience of assessment did your school want the children to have over the term? What actual impact/experience was there?	• • • • • •	What impact/ experience of assessment did you want the children to have over the term? What actual impact/experience was there?	• • • • •
Why? How do you know what you know? What did this look like?	• • • • • •	Why? How do you know what you know? What did this look like?	• • • • •
What impact/ experience of assessment does your school want pupils to have in the next term? What might this look like?	• • • • • •	What impact/ experience of assessment do you want pupils to have in the next term? What might this look like?	• • • • • •

Ways to take forward your thinking and your practice in the next term/year, based on your reflections above

• What key questions might you want to ask?

• What impact/experience of assessment do you want the children that you teach to have during their time with you? Why? What might this look like?

What next?

Further reading

Coe, R (2013) *Improving Education: A Triumph of Hope Over Experience*. Durham: Durham University Centre for Education and Monitoring.

Wiliam, D (2013) Assessment: The Bridge between Teaching and Learning. *Voices from the Middle*, 21(2): 15–20.

References

Assessment Reform Group (1999) *Assessment for Learning: Beyond the Black Box.* Cambridge: Cambridge School of Education.

Black, P, Harrison, C, Lee, C, Marshall, B, and Wiliam, D (2002) *Working Inside the Black Box – Assessment for Learning in the Classroom*. London: GL Assessment.

Black, P and Wiliam, D (1998) *Inside the Black Box: Raising Standards Through Classroom Assessment*. London: King's College School of Education.

Black, P and Wiliam, D (2006) *Assessment for Learning in the Classroom*. In Gardner, J (ed) *Assessment and Learning* (2nd ed) (pp 11–32). London: Sage.

Booth, N (2017) What Is Formative Assessment, Why Hasn't It Worked in Schools, and How Can We Make It Better in the Classroom? *Impact – Journal of the Chartered College of Teaching*. [online] Available at: https://impact.chartered.college/article/booth-what-formativ e-assessment-make-better-classroom (accessed 16 June 2019).

Christodoulou, D (2017) *Making Good Progress? The Future of Assessment for Learning.* Oxford: Oxford University Press.

Department for Education (DfE) (2015) *Final Report of the Commission on Assessment Without Levels*. London: The Stationery Office.

Goldstein, H and Leckie, G (2016) *The Evolution of School League Tables in England 1992– 2016: 'Contextual Value-Added', 'Expected Progress' and 'Progress 8'*. Bristol: Gradute School of Education.

Ofsted (2011) The Impact of the 'Assessing Pupils' Progress' Initiative. [online] Available at: www.gov.uk/government/publications/the-impact-of-the-assessing-pupils-progress-ini tiative (accessed 12 August 2019).

Chapter 2   Where are they going?

What? (The big idea) ◀◀◀

A 'backwards planning' approach

The 'backwards planning' approach became particularly prevalent in the 1990s, prompted by Wiggins and McTighe's 1998 book, *Understanding by Design*. The core idea behind this approach is that you start the planning process with the end point (ie where the planning will take you to) and work backwards from that point. It might help to think about this in terms of cooking a big meal for lots of guests: you start with the time that you want to eat and then work backwards from there as to when to put the potatoes in, what needs to be prepared in advance, right back to writing the shopping list for the ingredients needed. This approach has become a bedrock of Initial Teacher Training and the wider sector, underpinning planning from small in-lesson sequences to long-term plans for whole-school improvement.

Where a 'backwards planning' approach sits at the heart of a practical approach to assessment, it has the potential to inform your thinking and reflection about its place within the construction of learning for pupils. This chapter explores the links between assessment, planning and reflection in broad brushstrokes. It aims to highlight the importance of taking an holistic approach to assessment and to explore the idea that assessment is as much about 'how did they do it?' and 'how can they do it better?' as it is about 'how did they do?'. These three questions sit behind the reflective and practical tasks in this chapter.

So what? ◀ ◀ ◀

What difference will this make?

There are numerous factors which influence the thinking behind and content of planning, including but not limited to:

» frameworks provided in your setting;

» government priorities;

» meeting the needs of individuals;

» the programme of study;

» lesson length and frequency.

Behind all of this, though, there needs to be a considered approach to planning. This needs to be robust enough to maintain a resolute focus on excellent learning yet sufficiently flexible to survive the variations in context-driven practices. It is the constant focus on impact on pupils which should ultimately drive your planning and it is this which places assessment as a key factor in the process.

In a practical sense, there are two key ways in which assessment is integral to 'backwards planning'.

1. Knowing where you want pupils to end up (what are they working towards, what kind of assessment is attached to this and what assessment/learning context does this sit within?).

2. Using assessment as a reflective tool to assess the success of learning opportunities (this could be anything from at task level to a longer-term plan) to inform the planning of future learning (with a 'backwards' approach to reflection – see the **reflective task** and **case study** below for an example of this). This reflection can happen *during* the lesson as well as after it has taken place, giving it the potential to have 'live' impact on improving learning during the lesson.

In order to enable the second of these to take place successfully, it is key to consider a wide range of modes of assessment, exploring the full gamut of formative/developmental assessment approaches and developing an increasingly substantive 'toolkit' of these over time. However, quantity of strategies will only lead to a superficial approach to 'in-lesson' and 'between lesson' assessment. For this to be truly impactful, a truly reflective approach to assessment and planning is essential.

Thinking about reflective methodology as a way of considering your approaches to assessment, holistically drawing the planning elements together, will support you to think deeply about the efficacy of your approaches. This suggestion is intended as a 'masterly' approach to practice and to support your development of a flexible planning philosophy which has longevity centred around excellent learning for pupils. For the purposes of the examples below, Tripp's 'critical incident analysis' (1993) is the reflective approach used. You could also explore Kolb's Experiential Learning Cycle (1984), Brookfield's 'lenses' (1995) or a reflective approach from your ITT training/CPD in your setting as a way of thinking through these examples. This is not a 'one-size-fits-all' approach to reflective, assessment-informed, 'backwards' planning: indeed, it is about developing your pedagogical arsenal to be able to deploy the most effective model to ensure the best learning for pupils (more on this in later chapters).

Reflective task ◀◀◀

Apply the big idea to a practical situation in the classroom

Take a lesson from the past week and use the framework below to explore the roles of assessment and reflection in the planning cycle. Use the example below as a model, if you need to.

*Note: you don't have to use all of these rows – you can use more/less as needed.

Lesson chosen			What do you want to gain from this reflection and why (impact on pupils)?		
Assessment as reflection					
Moment in the lesson	How does this link with the moment preceding/ succeeding this?	How did pupils do?	How do you know what you know (evidence)? What assessment strategy did you use?	How did they do this?	How could they do this better?
What happened at the end of the lesson?					
What happened before/led to that?*					
What happened before/led to that?*					
What happened before/led to that?*					

What happened before/led to that?*						
What happened to start this off?						

Next steps – assessment-informed planning

What impact do you hope to have on pupils in the next lesson and why?		Key levers for success from this lesson to develop/adapt in future planning		Key opportunities for assessment next time	
End point for next lesson (you'll plan backwards from this)		How will you/pupils assess this?		How will you/pupils know whether they've been successful?	

Example Using the tool: creative writing

Lesson chosen	Creative writing – writing process – initial idea generation for own opening chapter for a fairy story.	What do you want to gain from this reflection and why (impact on pupils)?	I want to ascertain what the key blocks to pupils' idea generation are and plan to remove these in a subsequent lesson to improve writing skills.

Assessment as reflection

Moment in the lesson	How does this link with the moment preceding/ succeeding this?	How did pupils do?	How do you know what you know (evidence)? What assessment strategy did you use?	How did they do this?	How could they do this better?
What happened at the end of the lesson? Pupils undertook independent writing, fleshing out one to three of their ideas from their idea generation.	Pre – built on ideas generated in the thinking map exercise. Post – will lead into extending the draft and reviewing initial ideas and drafting the next lesson.	Some really struggled with getting ideas into full sentences – seemed to be more of an issue with their ideas than the writing per se. Most had a series of sentences created by the end of the lesson.	Pupil-teacher feedback – X commented 'But I don't know what to write about' despite having a range of ideas/words on their thinking map. There were a number of others who made comments to this effect. Y also said 'I'm worried my ideas aren't very good. It's boring' – again, echoed by three other pupils. Teacher observation – saw most pupils had a paragraph of prose.	Using the frameworks and scaffolds from earlier in the lesson.	Greater range of ideas from which to choose: need to create an idea generation context which leads pupils to have more confidence in their ideas to be able to get over this barrier to writing. Need to move them beyond the scaffold – embedding the drafting element of the writing process.

| What happened before/led to that?

Pupils created 'thinking maps' in response to a range of visual stimuli – independent task with peer talk to support. | Pre – individual task based on paired task: increasing independence and building on peer-created models.

Post – will lead into individual writing task: making idea generation significant. | All pupils had a range of ideas on their 'thinking maps' (at least six per picture). | Teacher observation – saw all pupils had lots of words/phrases as annotations for their images.

Pupil-teacher feedback – although they all had lots of annotations on their chosen images, at least one-third of pupils requested additional support/ feedback during the task. They were worried that none of their ideas were very good and X, Y, D and F all commented that 'it's boring' and 'I don't like my ideas'. | | Peer feedback could be framed by 'what's the idea you wish you'd had?' and 'what's the best idea you hear from someone else and why?', both to support pupils' confidence in their ideas and to leverage critical analysis (reading/ listening) skills for writing.

Teacher-pupil feedback needed to support pupils to see validity of ideas and to support quality over quantity – need to look at how the success criteria are couched for idea generation. |
|---|---|---|---|---|---|

| What happened to start this off?

Pupils worked in pairs to generate ideas in response to stimuli. | Pre – looked at models of opening chapters in the previous lesson and identified a series of key questions we ask as readers to look at what a quality opening needs to do.

Post – will lead into individual undertaking of the task: making idea generation significant. | All pupils had a range of ideas on their 'thinking maps' (at least six per picture). | Teacher observation – saw all pupils had lots of words/phrases as annotations for their images. | Paired talk, using talk framework based on questions developed by pupils in the previous lesson. | Could use the questions generated in the previous lesson as assessment framework for pupils feeding back on their own/ others' work – making use of 'mutually enhancing processes' (reading for writing).

Needed an assessment strategy to look at quality as well as quantity of ideas – links with the questioning idea above? |
|---|---|---|---|---|---|

Next steps – assessment-informed planning

What impact do you hope to have on pupils in the next lesson and why?	* Increase number of ideas from which pupils can create their drafts. * Increased pupil confidence in drafting stage. * Create opportunities for 'all ideas are potential good ideas' to remove barriers to writing.
Key levers for success from this lesson to develop/ adapt in future planning	* Pupil talk enabled the most successful outcomes in the lesson – need to exploit this further (see ideas above). * Pupils who were most successful were those with ideas with which they felt confidence (rather than number of ideas).

Key oppor-tunities for assessment next time	* *Peer feedback – using the ideas above.*
	* *Need to use teacher observation more effectively – too much focus on quantity of ideas rather than quality as a sign of success here.*
	* *How can pupils be doing more of the assessment in lessons? Need to move beyond the superficiality of the teacher observations in this lesson.*
End point for next lesson (you'll plan backwards from this)	* *Pupils have created opening paragraph which they've:*
	– used oral rehearsal to draft;
	– critically analysed with a peer;
	– used small group feedback to re-draft their paragraph.
How will you/ pupils assess this?	* *Shared with a small group for feedback.*
	* *Teacher 'live' feedback on drafts handed in.*
How will you/ pupils know whether they've been successful?	* *Pupils have a paragraph which they're confident to share with peers.*
	* *Range of pupil responses is broad and ideas have potential for development.*
	* *Pupils and I can see improved paragraphs from in-lesson feedback (range of techniques, improved impact on reader).*

Now what?

Practical ways to implement this in the classroom

The following tasks are intended to take the reflective approach a couple of steps further. They should challenge and support you in focusing on that key purpose of planning and assessment: maintaining a constant focus on ensuring excellent learning. 'Excellent learning' may require you to take pupils beyond 'the test' or the assessment; it may be a case of teaching beyond the confines of the test or the syllabus, taking pupils to what is excellent learning per se and then teaching them to 'play the game' of the test/assessment as part of a specific demonstration of the wider learning that they have undertaken.

Practical task for tomorrow ◀◀◀

Using your 'next steps' from the reflective task, review your plan for the next lesson with this group, using these points to examine the efficacy of the assessments you've planned and adapt if necessary.

Practical task for next week ◀◀◀

- Look at the week's lesson(s) for the same group that you identified for the reflective task.

- Plan one of/the lesson(s) for the week using the following prompts. These are an adaptation of the reflective framework.

- Review the lesson that you planned and taught using the following framework to evaluate the lesson and inform the next planning cycle.

Lesson overview (what's it about?)			What is the overall intended impact on pupils?		
Assessment-informed planning					
Where pupils need to be	How does this link with the moment preceding/succeeding this?	How will pupils do this?	What assessment strategy will you use? Why?	How will this help pupils to improve/move on?	Links to wider learning?
End of lesson					
Before this?					

▶▶

Before this?					
Before this?					
Before this?					
Start of this?					

Next steps – using assessment for reflection to inform planning					
What impact do you hope to have on pupils in the next lesson and why?		Key levers for success from this lesson to develop/ adapt in future planning		Key opportuni-ties for assessment next time	
End point for the next lesson (you'll plan backwards from this)		How will you/pupils assess this?		How will you/pupils know whether they've been successful?	

Practical task for the long term ◀◀◀

At the end of the current scheme/unit of work/medium-term plan for the group upon which you've already focused, review the learning and use this to inform your long-term planning using the following framework.

Scheme/unit of work/medium-term plan overview			What was the overall intended impact on pupils?		
Assessment as reflection					
Moment in the scheme/ unit of work/ medium-term plan	How does this link with the moment preceding/ succeeding this?	How did pupils do?	How do you know what you know (evidence)? What assessment strategies did you use?	How did they do this?	How could they do this better?
End of scheme/ unit of work/ medium-term plan					
Before this?					
Before this?					
Before this?					
Before this?					
Start of this?					

Next steps – using assessment for reflection to inform planning					
What impact do you hope to have on pupils by the end of the term/ year and why?		Key levers for success from this plan to develop/ adapt in future planning		Key opportuni- ties for assessment next time	
End point for term/ year/ external assessment (you'll plan backwards from this)		How will you/pupils assess this? What mile- stones can there be to bridge the gap between the end of the term/year and now?		How will you/pupils know whether they've been successful? How might pupils be successful beyond the outcomes of assess- ment(s) planned?	

What next? ◀ ◀ ◀

Further reading

Earl, L M and Katz, S (2006) *Rethinking Classroom Assessment with Purpose in Mind: Assessment for Learning, Assessment as Learning, Assessment of Learning*. Winnipeg, Manitoba: Crown in Right of Manitoba.

Wiggins, G and McTighe, J (2012) *Understanding by Design Framework*. Alexandria, VA: ASCD.

References

Brookfield, S (1995) *Becoming a Critically Reflective Teacher*. San Francisco, CA: Jossey-Bass.

Kolb, D A (1984) *Experiential Learning: Experience as the Source of Learning and Development*. Englewood Cliffs, NJ: Prentice-Hall, Inc.

Tripp, D (1993) *Critical Incidents in Teaching: Developing Professional Judgement*. London: Routledge.

Wiggins, G and McTighe, J (2005) *Understanding by Design* Expanded 2nd ed. Alexandria, VA: Association for Supervision and Curriculum Development.

Chapter 3   What, how, why and effects: assessing pupils' learning

What? (The big idea)

The six 'big questions'

Six 'big questions' underpin much of the thinking and practice outlined in the history of assessment presented in Chapter 1, which you could use to frame your work as a teacher and to focus that work on the impact on your pupils' learning. In essence, whether reflecting on a lesson, planning for a year's worth of curriculum or driving your own learning through professional development, the following could be used to shape your analytical, impact-focused thinking.

1. **'What?'** – what are you teaching? What's the focus of this lesson? What skill do pupils need to develop? What concept do pupils need to understand? What facts do pupils need to know?

2. **'How?'** – how might you teach this? How might pupils do these things? How

could you use pupils' prior learning? How can you implement this learning/ approach in the longer term?

3. **'Why?'** – why would I use this approach? (Do I agree with its purpose and intention?) Why do pupils need to do this? Why is this the approach you've chosen (as opposed to another)? Why is this learning important? How can pupils explore 'the why' (links with understanding) in the lesson through this?

4. **'Effects?'** – what impact do you intend to have on pupils?

5. **'How do you know what you know?'** – what does learning look like? How do you know that learning has/not taken place? How do you know whether the approach has been successful or not? What specific evidence/data/examples from pupils' learning could you cite?

6. **'So what?'** – what are the implications for your future practice? How can you implement these practices in the long term? How might this impact positively on pupils' learning in the future? How has this developed your professional skills, knowledge and understanding?

The above questions are predicated on an assumption that assessment has a formative, developmental function, based on the ideas outlined in Chapter 1. Indeed, this might suggest that 'assessment *for* learning' approaches have a key role to play within teaching and learning to enable pupils to progress in their learning.

Christodoulou (2017) addresses a facet of this thinking in *Making Good Progress? The Future of Assessment for Learning*. Among a consideration of school-wide approaches to rethinking assessment, Christodoulou (2017, p 21) notes that *'[assessment for learning] is not just about teachers being responsive; it is about pupils responding to information about their progress'*. In this way, assessment could become a dynamic teaching and learning tool, promoting a pupil-led (or, at least, pupil-centred) approach to both assessment and teaching and learning per se.

As outlined in Chapter 1, Booth's 2017 article for the Chartered College of Teaching's magazine, *Impact*, highlights several key strategies for dynamic use of assessment in teaching to enable and enhance pupils' learning.

In this chapter, you will have the opportunity to think about and experiment with a range of approaches based on the above ideas.

So what? ◀◀◀

What difference will it make?

The practical approaches in this chapter are an opportunity to reflect on and develop your classroom practice, using impact on pupils' learning as a key tool to do this. The thinking and 'doing' in this chapter link with the ideas in Chapter 5: it is an opportunity to think about 'pupil data' and 'pupil impact' in a number of ways to develop your professional practice for, and understanding of, assessment.

The reflective task here is a revised version of the reflective task in Chapter 1: it is intended to take your thinking from that point further (though it will also be useful if you're looking at this chapter first) as well as preparing you for the practical tasks in the 'now what?' section that follows.

The key aim of this task is to explore how you are implementing your understanding of what 'assessment' means to you as a teacher. Over time, and through the work that you'll do as part of this and other chapters in this book, you could use these 'framing' questions as a starting point for on-going development of your professional understanding and practical use of assessment. This reflective task is a good place to start with this.

There are three broad questions underpinning this task.

1. What influences your ideas about and approaches to assessment?

2. What impact does assessment have on the children that you teach?

3. How does this influence the ways in which you and pupils use assessment in your classroom?

Reading	Feedback from colleagues	Feedback from pupils
What have you learned?	What have you learned?	What have you learned?
How does this influence your practice?	How does this influence your practice?	How does this influence your practice?
Impact on your learning?	Impact on your learning?	Impact on your learning?
Why?	Why?	Why?
How could pupils use assessment based on what you've learned?	How could pupils use assessment based on what you've learned?	How could pupils use assessment based on what you've learned?
Impact on pupils' learning?	Impact on pupils' learning?	Impact on pupils' learning?
Why?	Why?	Why?
Training you've had	**ASSESSMENT**	**Curricula/specifications/ frameworks**
What have you learned?	• What does it mean to me?	What have you learned?
How does this influence your practice?	• What influences my ideas about and approaches to assessment?	How does this influence your practice?
Impact on your learning?		Impact on your learning?
Why?	• What impact does assessment have on the children that I teach?	Why?
How could pupils use assessment based on what you've learned?	• How does this influence the ways in which I and my pupils use assessment in my classroom?	How could pupils use assessment based on what you've learned?
Impact on pupils' learning?		Impact on pupils' learning?
Why?		Why?
Tests/assessments	**Observations of others**	**Other (anything else)**
What have you learned?	What have you learned?	What have you learned?
How does this influence your practice?	How does this influence your practice?	How does this influence your practice?
Impact on your learning?	Impact on your learning?	Impact on your learning?
Why?	Why?	Why?
How could pupils use assessment based on what you've learned?	How could pupils use assessment based on what you've learned?	How could pupils use assessment based on what you've learned?
Impact on pupils' learning?	Impact on pupils' learning?	Impact on pupils' learning?
Why?	Why?	Why?

Example   Using the reflective task

This example looks at one of the eight focus areas from the reflective task.

Training you've had

What have you learned?

- The session looked at using quick approaches to gauge confidence in what's been the focus of a lesson. This seemed to be about both checking that pupils felt confident and also identifying which children might need to be prioritised for interventions (in the next part of the lesson/next lesson etc) to address confidence.

How does this influence your practice?

- I could use the 'traffic lights' (red for not at all confident, amber for unsure, green for confident) during the transitions in a lesson to check on pupils' readiness for the next part of the learning. I might need to think about using the teaching assistant in my lesson to provide more capacity or to look at resources which might help pupils to support themselves/peers.

Impact on your learning?

- It's made me think about the role that confidence might have on pupils' readiness to learn and how this might be a barrier to their progress.

Why?

- Until now I have focused on using assessments that 'test' whether pupils have learned something and/or can do something. I am now thinking about how to link what pupils have actually learned with how they feel about their learning. This might also be useful for thinking about the kind of atmosphere pupils need to learn best for a given lesson/activity.

How could pupils use assessment based on what you've learned?

- Pupils could be more involved in thinking about their own learning by using the strategy outlined above. They could use this assessment of their confidence to think about why they do/don't feel confident and link this to what they've learned.

Impact on pupils' learning?

- I can evaluate the sorts of activities which leave pupils feeling most confident about their learning. If I work out what these tend to look like, I can use them to build pupils' confidence across lessons.

I could use pupils' confidence as a way of extending their learning – I could plan to gradually enable pupils to be confident in going beyond where they are secure in their learning to accelerate their learning.

Pupils start to see the links between their learning and how they feel about their learning.

Why?

Being aware of pupils' confidence and competence will enable me to plan in more depth to differentiate for ability and confidence, using in-lesson information from this kind of approach.

Now what?

Practical ways to implement this in the classroom

In this section, you can explore some ideas for assessment in your classroom. The concepts shared here are based on the ideas in Booth and Christodoulou's work, with the intention being that you can both see and explore what this thinking might look like in practice.

For each of the ideas shared here, the following will be outlined and framed.

- The rationale behind the idea/activity/strategy.

- What to do and ideas for how to do it (linking to questions 1 and 2 of the six 'big questions' from earlier on in this chapter).

- Reflective prompt questions for you to analyse the use of that approach (linking to questions 3–6 of the six 'big questions' from earlier on in this chapter).

You do not need to try these approaches in the order that they are presented here: you could use your thinking from the reflective task above to prioritise where you start and/or to make adaptations to the ideas that follow.

Approach	Learning intentions shared with the class
Before teaching	
Rationale	'A common feature within classroom practice today is the sharing of learning intentions (also known as learning objectives) with students where the intended learning behind the tasks and activities is revealed. The clarification and understanding, at student level, of learning intentions, however, is essential so that students become able to hold a concept similar to that of the teacher (Sadler, 1989). Writing good learning intentions, though, is hard as we need to distinguish clearly in our planning not only what the students will be doing, but what they will be learning by doing it' (Booth, 2017).
During teaching	

What to do and **how** to do it	• Try this approach in *one* of your lessons tomorrow.
	 • This approach makes explicit use of the 'learning intention(s)' for a lesson. When devising the learning intention, you could ask yourself:
	   – Is it based on what pupils should know, understand or be able to do?
	   – Is it focused on what pupils are learning (rather than doing)?
	   – Is it focused on the process of learning (rather than the task or end outcome)?
	   – Does it encourage pupils to think about their learning?
	   – Is it something that pupils can respond to on a personal level?
	   – Is it meaningful, clear and understandable by learners?

- Suggested approach to try:

  - At the start of the lesson, share the learning intention(s) with the group.

  - Pupils respond to the learning intention: what will be the things that they will need to do to demonstrate the intending learning? What skills will they need to use/develop? What knowledge/understanding will they need to use/develop?

  - How might this approach link with the idea of using success criteria (see below) as an approach to assessment?

  - At each transition point in the lesson (ie the end of each input and/or task), you revisit the learning intention and pupils' initial responses to the questions about their meeting of it. How far have they come so far? What do they now need to do/use/develop?

  - The plenary focuses on an 'end of the lesson' review of pupils' starting points viz. the learning intention(s) and their reflection on this learning at this point. The final questions asked of pupils at this stage (to link the lesson's learning to future lessons): 1) Key learning from today in relation to the learning intention? 2) What's the one thing that you still need to develop and why (linking back to the learning intention)?

- Possible adaptations to think about:

  - How might reversing this process enable you/pupils to check on whether the intended learning has taken place? How might this also be an opportunity for pupils to think about *how* their learning has taken place (metacognition)?

After teaching – reflecting on your practice

'Big question'	Supporting prompt questions
Why?	• What did you intend to achieve by using this approach in this lesson?
	• Why was this learning important?
	• How did pupils explore 'the why' (links with understanding) in the lesson through this?

Effects?	• What impact did you intend to have on pupils?
	• What impact did you actually have on pupils?
How do you know what you know?	• What did learning look like in the lesson?
	• How do you know that learning did/did not take place?
	• How do you know whether the approach was successful or not?
	• What specific evidence/data/examples from pupils' learning do you have from using this approach in the lesson?
So what?	• What are the implications for your future practice, based on your reflections?
	• How could you implement these practices in the long term?
	• Why and how might this impact positively on pupils' learning in the future?
	• How could you use the *principles* of the approach you used here but do things in a different way? Why?
	• How has this developed your professional skills, knowledge and understanding?

Practical task for next week ◀◀◀

Approach	'Live' marking/feedback
Before teaching	
Rationale	'The notion of any kind of feedback, according to Sadler (1989), is powerful for several reasons:
	1. It informs teachers about levels of knowledge, understanding and skills attained or yet to be attained by the student
	2. It aims to facilitate learners in being able to identify and amend a gap in learning

| | 3. *It assists teachers in reducing and selecting suitable tasks or activities, and* |
| | 4. *It allows teachers to modify their teaching in order to support the closing of the gap'* (Booth, 2017). |

What to do and **how** to do it	• Try this approach in *three* of your lessons next week (this could be across several different classes [secondary], the same subject over three lessons in which learning is cumulative [EY and primary], different topics [all phases], the same skill in several different lessons [all phases], or based on any other premise useful to your pupils).
	• Pupils get 'real-time', instant feedback on their work in the lesson. This could be: written feedback on written work; solutions to problems; visual feedback (ticks, stickers, stamps, etc) on work in books, on worksheets, etc; questions written on work to extend their learning further.
	• Suggested approach to try (explained through an example in practice – primary mathematics):
	– Key methodology for solving the problem is modelled by the teacher to the whole class.
	– Children complete a worked example as a whole class.
	– Children are given a set of problems to solve, using what has been demonstrated during the whole-class sequence.
	– During the independent task, the teacher goes round the class, providing 'instant' feedback as pupils work. This feedback: highlights errors and correct answers; provides an opportunity to identify misconceptions and whether these are common (to groups and/or the class) or pertinent to individuals.
	– Where misconceptions are isolated to individual children, the teacher addresses these during the live marking.

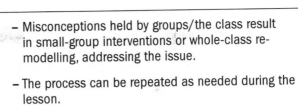

- Misconceptions held by groups/the class result in small-group interventions or whole-class re-modelling, addressing the issue.

- The process can be repeated as needed during the lesson.

- This process replaces post-lesson marking for the lesson.

• Possible adaptations to think about:

- How could you use non-verbal and/or oral feedback in response to practical work, such as performances, demonstrating a skill in PE, behaviours?

- How might pupils use this approach for peer-assessment?

After teaching – reflecting on your practice

'Big question'	Supporting prompt questions
Why?	• What did you intend to achieve by using this approach in these lessons?
	• Why was this learning important?
	• How did pupils explore 'the why' (links with understanding) in the lesson through this?
Effects?	• What impact did you intend to have on pupils?
	• What impact did you actually have on pupils?
	• Was the use of this approach more successful in some lessons than others? Why? Why not?
How do you know what you know?	• What did learning look like in these lessons?
	• How do you know that learning did/did not take place?
	• How do you know whether the approach was successful or not?
	• What specific evidence/data/examples from pupils' learning do you have from using this approach in these lessons?

So what?	• What are the implications for your future practice, based on your reflections?
	• How could you implement these practices in the long term?
	• Why and how might this impact positively on pupils' learning in the future?
	• How could you use the *principles* of the approach you used here but do things in a different way? Why?
	• How has this developed your professional skills, knowledge and understanding?

Practical task for the long term ◀◀◀

This task is split into two levels of planning.

• Planning for the use of assessment in the medium term.

• Planning for the use of assessment in the long term.

Medium-term planning (ie a 'unit of work', 'topic' area, half-term/term)

Approach	Success criteria
Before teaching	
Rationale	'Sharing what success looks like with students is at the very heart of formative assessment and provides regular opportunities for such assessment to take place throughout the lesson. As one student puts it, knowing and understanding the success criteria is "like knowing the teacher's secret" (Spendlove, 2009: 18). Within formative assessment, success criteria can act as an aide memoire to students throughout the lesson so that, through on-going reflection, their learning can be kept on track. The regular referral to success criteria also allows teachers to engage in conversations with their students where meaningful oral feedback is given on where the learner is now, where they need to be, and how they are going to get there' (Booth, 2017).

Why?	• What's the purpose of using this approach?
	• What's the intention behind it?
	• Why is this the approach you've chosen (as opposed to another) for this planning?
	• Why do pupils need to do this?
	• Why is this learning important?
	• How could pupils explore 'the why' (links with understanding) in the lesson through this?
Effects?	• What impact do you intend to have on pupils?
How do you know what you know?	• What do you expect the learning to look like?
What to do and **how** to do it – *planning*	• Try this approach for your medium-term planning for *one* strand of your teaching (this could be one focus across several different classes [secondary], one class over a half-term/term [secondary], the same subject over several weeks of lessons in which learning is cumulative [EY and primary], a single topic [all phases], the same skill in several different lessons [all phases], or based on any other premise useful to your pupils).
	• This approach makes explicit use of 'success criteria' for learning. When devising these success criteria, you could ask yourself:
	– Are there clear, relevant and measurable definitions of success?
	– Is it clear how the teacher and pupils will know they have been successful in the learning?
	– Do they use words that emphasise knowing, learning, thinking or using skills?
	– Are they linked with the learning intention(s) but also distinct?
	– Do they highlight what evidence of learning is anticipated?
	– Have they been developed with pupils? Why?
	– How are they going to be used at the centre of feedback?

What to do and **how** to do it – *delivery*	• Suggested approaches to try (explained through examples in practice – primary art and secondary [Key Stage 4] mathematics, though both are adaptable for other phases and subjects): – *Key Stage 4 mathematics – focus on using the retrospective generation of success criteria to help pupils prepare for external tests.* For different methods of written calculations, use the method on mini-whiteboards. Following this, pupils write success criteria for these methods on A3 paper. This becomes an explicit process of how to 'do' that method of calculation. Display these 'success processes' in the classroom and prompt pupils to refer back to them when using these methods in lessons (this is similar to the 'working walls' seen in many primary schools). Use the same principles of 'retrospective generation' of success criteria to support pupils' GCSE preparation as part of using specimen/past test papers. After pupils have completed a past paper, hand the papers back and go through the papers with pupils. At the centre of this, pupils devise a list of success criteria for the mathematics GCSE. Prompt pupils to include all of the feedback from the past paper work. Before the next specimen/past paper, revisit the success criteria generated following the previous paper and use these as a starting point for assessing pupils' work on these. – *Primary drama – focus on using success criteria to generate a quality performance.* Children have been working on *War Horse* by Michael Morpurgo and this lesson is intended to explore the context of the book through the use of tableaux and thought-tracking.

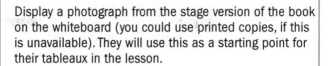

Display a photograph from the stage version of the book on the whiteboard (you could use printed copies, if this is unavailable). They will use this as a starting point for their tableaux in the lesson.

Explain to the children that the photograph is a model of what you would like them to produce for their tableaux. Ask the children to analyse their photograph: what are the people doing? Why are they doing this? How does this link with what they've read in class so far in terms of the book? In this discussion, communicate how you are thinking about the photograph to model this process.

Then, ask the children to tell you what the success criteria could be for creating a good tableau. In other words, how will they reproduce the quality of the photograph in their own work?

Use the success criteria from this sequence to provide feedback on the tableaux that each group shares.

Repeat the process with the success criteria for 'good thought-tracking', linking this both to the performance technique and pupils' reading of the book.

At the end of the lesson, when all groups have shared their thought-tracked tableaux, use the success criteria for children to reflect on their own and other's work.

• Possible adaptations to think about – either during your teaching as you respond to pupils' emerging learning and/or as part of your reflections:

  – How could pupils more overtly construct the success criteria? How might this be both demonstrative of their learning and a way of assessing further development needs?

  – How might success criteria provide a scaffold for learning?

  – How could you adapt/build on these approaches for your pupils?

  – How might these approaches link with peer- and self-assessment (below)?

After teaching – reflecting on your practice	
'Big question'	**Supporting prompt questions**
Effects?	• What impact did you have on pupils?
How do you know what you know?	• What did learning look like? • How do you know that learning did/did not take place? • How do you know whether the approach was successful or not? • What specific evidence/data/examples from pupils' learning could you cite?
So what?	• What are the implications for your future practice? • How can you implement these practices in the long term? • Why might this impact positively on pupils' learning in the future? • How could you use the *principles* of what you/the pupils did here but do things in a different way? Why? • How has this developed your professional skills, knowledge and understanding?

Long-term planning (ie an academic year, examination specification duration, key stage)

Approach	Using peer- and self-assessment
Before teaching	
Rationale	*'Peer- and self-assessment "is essential to learning because students can only achieve a learning goal if they understand that goal and can assess what they need to do to reach it" (Black and Wiliam, 2006: 15). Within the understanding of formative assessment, what this means is that the students know what to do to develop each other's, as well as their own, learning.*

	The interaction between these key strategies not only fosters engaging learning environments, but also makes clear to both teachers and students that learning is, indeed, heading in the intended direction. The information these strategies elicit is then used to decide what to do next. This is formative assessment in action' (Booth, 2017).
Why?	• What's the purpose of using this approach? • What's the intention behind it? • Why is this the approach you've chosen (as opposed to another) for this planning? • Why do pupils need to do this? • Why is this learning important? • How could pupils explore 'the why' (links with understanding) in the lesson through this?
Effects?	• What impact do you intend to have on pupils?
How do you know what you know?	• What do you expect the learning to look like?
What to do and **how** to do it – *planning*	• Try this approach for your long-term planning for *one* strand of your teaching (this could be one focus across several different classes [secondary], one class over a half-term/term [secondary], the same subject over several weeks of lessons in which learning is cumulative [EY and primary], a single topic [all phases], the same skill in several different lessons [all phases], or based on any other premise useful to your pupils).

| **What** to do and **how** to do it – *delivery* | • Suggested approaches to try:

   – *Peer-assessment*

As a routine for feedback in lessons, pupils use the following 'focus questions for listening'. These are used throughout lessons as a way of both framing listening in talk-based activities and to develop pupils' peer–peer communication skills in a positive way.

  What's the best idea someone had and why?

  What's the idea you wish you'd had and why?

  Who's asked the best question and why?

  Who's shown/said/shared something you didn't know before? How has this helped you learn?

  What's the best use of a word [this lesson/today/this week] and why?

  What's been the best use of [insert relevant skill] and why?

  – *Self-assessment*

The intentions of this approach are: a) for pupils to use feedback dynamically to develop their work for an extended piece of learning/an extended task; b) for pupils to also have a tangible sense of the progress that they have made over time. This model is easily adaptable for a shorter time frame (ie it could be used in a single lesson for the development of a skill/response).

Over time, pupils revisit their work. This is framed by the use of success criteria, ideally developed as part of this process. The number of steps in the middle part of this process can be increased, depending in the intended scale of the learning.

  – Step 1 – pupils *review* their work using the success criteria. They identify a maximum of three specific aspects of success. They identify a maximum of three specific things to improve. With teacher/peer support if needed, pupils record *how* they will do these things, *why* and what this *will look like* when they've been successful.

  – Step 2 – pupils *revise* their work based on their self-assessment, 'doing' the things that they've identified. |

- Step 3 – pupils *review* their work using the success criteria *and* focusing on their identified areas for improvement. They identify a maximum of three specific aspects of success. They identify a maximum of three specific things to improve: if they have not addressed the improvements identified in the previous review, they refine the comments on *how* they will do these things, *why* and what this *will look like* when they've been successful (with teacher/peer support, if needed).

- Step 4 – pupils *revise* their work further, based on their self-assessment, 'doing' the things that they've identified.

- Step 5 – pupils undertake a 'final' assessment of their work, using the success criteria. They identify: a maximum of three specific aspects of success (*'how they know what they know'*); *what* that they have improved on the most; *how* they made this progress; *why* they have made this progress; the key thing that they have learned (*impact/effect*); how they will take this learning forward into the next unit/task/term/year (*'so what?'*).

• Possible adaptations to think about– either during your teaching as you respond to pupils' emerging learning and/or as part of your reflections:

- How might peer- and self-assessment be translated into peer- and self-directed learning?

- How might you combine the approaches above to include elements of peer- and self-assessment? Why? Potential impact?

- How does this link with the other approaches in this chapter? Why? How might thinking about these possible links develop your understanding of assessment and your practical approaches to assessment in your classroom?

'Big question'	Supporting prompt questions
Effects?	• What impact did you have on pupils?
How do you know what you know?	• What did learning look like? • How do you know that learning did/did not take place? • How do you know whether the approach was successful or not? • What specific evidence/data/examples from pupils' learning could you cite?
So what?	• What are the implications for your future practice? • How can you implement these practices in the long term? • Why might this impact positively on pupils' learning in the future? • How could you use the *principles* of what you/the pupils did here but do things in a different way? Why? • How has this developed your professional skills, knowledge and understanding?

What next?

Further reading

Glow Scotland (2014) Clarifying and Sharing Learning Intentions and Success Criteria. [online] Available at: https://blogs.glowscotland.org.uk/er/EastRenfrewshireLAR/files/2014/02/Clarifying_and_Sharing_LIs__SC.pdf (accessed 12 August 2019).

Spendlove, D (2009) *Putting Assessment for Learning into Practice*. London: Continuum.

Stewart, W (2012) Think You've Implemented Assessment for Learning? *Times Educational Supplement*. [online] Available at: www.tes.com/news/tes-archive/tes-publication/think-youve-implemented-assessment-learning (accessed 16 June 2019).

References

Black, P and Wiliam, D (2006) Assessment for Learning in the Classroom. In Gardner, J (ed) *Assessment and Learning* (2nd ed) (pp 11–32). London: Sage.

Booth, N (2017) What Is Formative Assessment, Why Hasn't It Worked in Schools, and How Can We Make It Better in the Classroom? *Impact – Journal of the Chartered College of Teaching*. [online] Available at: https://impact.chartered.college/article/booth-what-formativ e-assessment-make-better-classroom (accessed 16 June 2019).

Christodoulou, D (2017) *Making Good Progress? The Future of Assessment for Learning*. Oxford: Oxford University Press.

Glow Scotland (2014) Clarifying and Sharing Learning Intentions and Success Criteria. [online] Available at: https://blogs.glowscotland.org.uk/er/EastRenfrewshireLAR/ files/2014/02/Clarifying_and_Sharing_Lls__SC.pdf (accessed 21 March 2019).

Sadler, R (1989) Formative Assessment and the Design of Instructional Systems. *Instructional Science*, 18: 119–44.

Spendlove, D (2009) *Putting Assessment for Learning into Practice*. London: Continuum.

Chapter 4   Progress over time

What? (The big idea)

'Progress over time' is a phrase used frequently in Initial Teacher Training, in government and Ofsted documentation, and in the discussions of pupils' attainment in schools. Most usually, this phrase is used to refer to the quantitative data (based on internal and/or external summative assessments) gathered and tracked in schools which is used for both in-school target-setting and as part of external scrutiny. League tables, government success measures for schools and Ofsted (external data only under the Inspection Framework from 2019 onwards) all use this data to look at 'value added' by schools and at how 'well' pupils in any given school perform in comparison with the rest of the country/local area. This kind of 'progress data' measures individuals and cohorts against established starting points, giving a form of 'quality' judgement based on numerically calculated 'point scores' and their movement/lack thereof. An example of this would be the 'Progress 8' score introduced in England in 2016. In this progress score (usually between –1 and +1), pupils' attainment across a selected set of eight subjects from the end of primary (age 11, at the end of Key Stage 2) to the end of secondary (age 16, at the end of Key Stage 4) education is measured: a school's 'Progress 8' score is calculated as an average of its pupils' scores.

As part of this discussion, an overarching understanding of 'qualitative' and 'quantitative' data is useful:

Type of data	What is it?	How is it typically collected?	How is it typically analysed?
Quantitative	Numerically represented data. Can assume a 'measurable' quality to the information being collected. This kind of data tends to seek to define a given thing.	Through measuring things, usually numerical values/ quantities of things, usually through testing.	Through numerical comparisons and statistical analyses.
Qualitative	Data that characterises rather than measures. This kind of data tends to seek to describe a quality/ attributes.	Through observations, reflections, interviews, etc (ie pupil questionnaires).	Through themes/ descriptions and tends to be reported in prose.

Adapted from Minichiello (1990, p 5)

It is likely that you will have come across the idea of 'progress over time' during your Initial Teacher Training/teaching qualification assessment: the use of examples of your impact on pupils' learning and attainment is central to looking at the quality of trainees' teaching practice over time. In this context, you may have been asked to use data/evidence of pupils' qualitative and quantitative progress as part of the evidence that you presented for your assessment for Qualified Teacher Status (QTS). This may have included: photographs of pupils' work; examples of the impact of your feedback on pupils' work; scored assessment/test data; examples of pupils' oral contributions in lessons etc. The 'over time' is likely to have been the duration of a practical placement, over a series of lessons and/or over a specified learning period (ie a Scheme of Learning or the project for the half-term). The main purpose of presenting this material, as well as being evidence of your understanding of some forms of assessment, was to demonstrate the impact of your teaching on pupils' learning.

The key idea behind both the QTS assessment and the school judgement use of 'pupil progress', as captured in Ofsted's past documentation, is that high-quality teaching results in pupils making *'substantial and sustained progress'* (Ofsted, 2018). The definition of 'substantial and sustained progress' is one example of the opacity of what might be meant by 'progress over time'. The quality of pupils' progress is used as a key discriminator of quality of teaching and learning yet it has a range of possible measures which, as Ofsted themselves noted in the former iterations of both their *Initial Teacher Education Inspection Handbook* (2015, p 32; updated 2018) and *School Inspection Handbook* (2018, pp 58–63), may need to be subject to the caveat of context (ie variations in starting-point context, SEND and other factors). It is interesting to note that neither of these handbooks specified any kind of timescale over which this progress might be measured and neither provided a suggested period/context for this. There was an implicit sense in which this may be seen as an assumed understanding, both in terms of 'progress' and the idea of this being over a 'sustained' period of time. This links back to those external measures of 'progress over time' outlined above and, most particularly, the values which are published as part of league tables and government quality markers.

This 'big picture' may initially seem remote from the everyday work of teachers in their classrooms. However, it is the external context which affects your classroom and what you are hoping to achieve with and for your pupils on a daily basis. Developing an understanding of this might support you in constructing your own approach to planning for, tracking and assessment of 'progress over time'.

So what? ◀ ◀ ◀

What difference will it make?

In almost all examples of progress measures used across the education piste, the data used to inform these are largely quantitative, suitable for inclusion in a spreadsheet and linked with some form of marked, summative assessment. A key exception to this is the tracking in early years education which, by the very nature of the key learning and skills development in that age range, focuses on qualitative progress measures necessitated by human childhood development markers. This focus on social skills, fundamental physical development, language acquisition and proficiency building might usefully have a wider application across the educational timeline: these skills remain fundamental to cognitive development and curricular success, despite the foci for assessment changing. A focus on pupils' confidence levels (as well as their competency), social skills and the core underlying learning skills of listening and speaking might not only support but accelerate and enhance pupils' progress, in both the short and long term.

The ideas of this in practice might be most easily and impactfully seen in approaches focused on 'talk for learning'. This world of educational theory is based on the premise that talk is fundamental to cognition, learning and communication:

> *Children, we now know, need to talk, and to experience a rich diet of spoken language, in order to think and to learn. Reading, writing and number may be the acknowledged curriculum 'basics' but talk is arguably the true foundation of learning.*
>
> (Alexander, 2004, p 5)

Robin Alexander's (2004) work on 'dialogic teaching' is one of the best-known examples of this pedagogy. This approach *'emphasises dialogue through which pupils learn to reason, discuss, argue, and explain, in order to develop their higher order thinking and articulacy'* (Jay et al, 2017, p 6). The impact of this approach on pupils' 'progress over time' was explored by the Education Endowment Foundation's 2017 evaluation report, which examined the impact of a dialogic teaching approach on primary pupils' attainment in English, science and mathematics. The key conclusions of the project were that children who were part of the approach made *'two additional months' progress in English and science, and one additional month's progress in maths, compared to children in control schools, on average'* (Jay et al, 2017, p 44). Children eligible for free school meals (FSM) made even more progress, making two additional months' progress in all three subjects compared with children in the same group in the control schools.

In short, for 'progress over time' to have true meaning and purpose, you may need to consider what you are tracking, and how and why you are tracking progress. This understanding of 'progress' perhaps needs to consider the harder to measure progress that pupils make: qualities such as confidence, engagement and enjoyment may be vital to pupils' overall successes but may need to be tracked (or, at least, noted) in order to maximise their impact and importance. How might this enable you to see progress which might seem invisible or insignificant within the context of grades/marks? How might this support you in identifying strengths for all pupils, seeing the layers of their potential and attainment and perhaps reframing what 'success' can look like? We'll explore these ideas further in Chapter 5.

Reflective task ◀◀◀

Apply the big idea to a practical situation in the classroom

There are several key questions that the ideas in the chapter present for you as an early career practitioner.

1. What does 'progress over time' mean to me and in my context? What measure of progress am I using?

2. What kinds of assessment data/evidence should (or could) I be collecting?

3. Why and how is this data useful? Is it for the assessment of my performance as teacher? Is it for my own use to reflect on the efficacy of my practice? How might it serve both purposes while also accelerating pupils' progress?

4. How might this thinking about the kinds of assessment data influence my thinking about the core pedagogical approaches in my classroom?

5. What qualitative and quantitative impact do I want to have on my pupils?

Either with your mentor or as part of your own reflection, explore these questions.

You'll link to this thinking for the reflective task in Chapter 5 (though it is not a prerequisite to have done the task above, it will support the depth of your thinking in that chapter).

Example   Using the tool

The example explored here takes the answers to Question 1 in the reflective task above to be that the focus is on children being 'next-year ready'. The example that follows here is just one possible example of a worked response to that question. Other examples of 'what measure of progress am I using?' could include: specified increase in assessment/test scores; social skill development (especially in early years); links to readiness for GCSE content (for Key Stage 3 pupils); level and frequency of interventions needed over time.

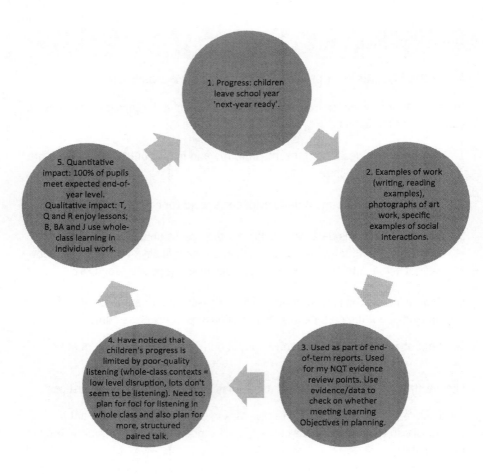

1. Progress: children leave school year 'next-year ready'.

2. Examples of work (writing, reading examples), photographs of art work, specific examples of social interactions.

3. Used as part of end-of-term reports. Used for my NQT evidence review points. Use evidence/data to check on whether meeting Learning Objectives in planning.

4. Have noticed that children's progress is limited by poor-quality listening (whole-class contexts = low level disruption, lots don't seem to be listening). Need to: plan for foci for listening in whole class and also plan for more, structured paired talk.

5. Quantitative impact: 100% of pupils meet expected end-of-year level. Qualitative impact: T, Q and R enjoy lessons; B, BA and J use whole-class learning in individual work.

Now what? ◀◀◀

Practical ways to implement this in the classroom

Practical task for tomorrow ◀◀◀

In at least one lesson, select three pupils for whom quantitative progress may seem minimal/below expectations. Focus on in-lesson progress for these pupils in terms of the following skills/qualities:

- confidence;

- enjoyment;

- engagement;

- peer–peer talk;

- listening;

- whole-class contributions.

Practical task for next week ◀◀◀

For one of the pupils identified above:

- select one of the skills/qualities from the list above. This should be the one in which you feel that they are least proficient and/or which might make the most difference to their learning experience;

- plan for opportunities to focus on the development of this quality in the following week's lessons;

- make a note of the progress that this pupil makes over the week.

Practical task for the long term ◀◀◀

Consider your learning from the tasks above: revisit the 'reflection task' questions above, using this experience as an example on which to further develop your thinking.

What next? ◀ ◀ ◀

Further reading

Alexander, R J (2003) *Talk for Learning: The First Year*. Northallerton: North Yorkshire County Council.

Alexander, R J (2005) *Teaching Through Dialogue: The First Year*. London: Barking and Dagenham Council.

Alexander, R J (2005) *Talk for Learning: The Second Year*. Northallerton: North Yorkshire County Council.

Andrews, J (2017) *The Introduction of Progress 8.* London: Centre Forum.

Gill, T (2017) *The Impact of the Introduction of Progress 8 on the Uptake and Provision of Qualifications in English Schools*. Cambridge Assessment Research Report. Cambridge: Cambridge Assessment.

References

Alexander, R (2004) *Towards Dialogic Teaching: Rethinking Classroom Talk*. Cambridge: Dialogos.

Ofsted (2015; updated September 2018) *Initial Teacher Education Inspection Handbook*. Manchester: Ofsted.

Ofsted (2018) *School Inspection Handbook*. Manchester: Ofsted.

Jay, T, Willis, B, Thomas, P, Taylor, R, Moore, N, Burnett, C, Merchant, G and Stevens, A (2017) *Dialogic Teaching: Evaluation Report and Executive Summary*. London: Education Endowment Foundation.

Minichiello, V (1990) *In-Depth Interviewing: Researching People*. Melbourne: Longman Cheshire.

Chapter 5 Capturing progress: what lies behind the spreadsheet?

What? (The big idea)

Building on the ideas in Chapter 4, this chapter is a further exploration of key thinking around qualitative and quantitative progress measures for young people in schools. This chapter also explores cross-phase and cross-curricular learning, supporting you to critically reflect on learning from the whole curriculum and learning continuum to develop high-quality, developmental approaches to assessing your pupils in a range of ways.

Qualitative and quantitative progress measures

We've seen in Chapter 4 that external progress measures have a tendency to focus on quantitative data, with examples such as the Progress 8 measure used in England as an established system. This kind of quantitative, numerically calculated data which looks at performance relative to the individual, an in-school and a local/national cohort very much sits at the centre of data generation, monitoring and analysis in educational settings. In essence, the difference between these two kinds of measures might be aligned with formative and summative assessment (see Chapter 1): qualitative progress might most naturally be a result of and/ or monitored through formative assessment modes; quantitative progress and attainment might be most easily demonstrated through summative assessments.

While many educational practitioners use qualitative data as part of their practice, this can seem more useful in the shorter term (ie in-lesson assessment and progress tracking) rather than the longer term. This may be as a result of the challenges in capturing and, ultimately, tracking this kind of data. Key questions such as 'how do you measure confidence?' and 'how do you capture levels of enjoyment?' are important and present challenges both in terms of definition and the ways in which we might represent these as calculable measures. Perhaps more useful questions in relation to qualitative data and their subsequent progress measures might be to consider 'what impact might focusing on this aspect of pupils' learning have on their progress and success?' and 'why might this kind of progress tracking support quantitative progress tracking?'.

Cross-phase and cross-curricular learning

The vast majority of schools organise their pupils in horizontal learning groups, with the grouping at a cohort level being driven by age and any other sub-groups (such as grouping by ability, subject choice, etc) coming out of this main grouping. Similarly, key data sets for analysing assessment outcomes tend to be organised in such a way: with key points in the chronological careers of learners as the key factor for the set and any other identifiers (FSM, LAC, Pupil Premium, SEND, etc) existing as sub-sets of the data. This approach does facilitate analysis which looks at trends of performance for identified groups. This is used by schools, educational institutions, the government and inspection bodies as part of their analysis of the successes and areas for development in the provision offered by a given establishment.

If you were to consider education as a continuum, rather than a series of chronological steps to be 'passed', what opportunities might this raise for how you view progress? What might you think about the kind of progress you want to track and the ways in which you might measure this? That is not to say that you should, or can, ignore the frameworks already in place for this. You will be working in a setting in which there are set frameworks for assessing, tracking, analysing and reporting on pupils' progress and outcomes. This is important and they are mechanisms with which you need to become familiar, increasingly confident and adept at using. However, that is not the whole story: as we've explored elsewhere in this book, the purposes of and uses for assessment are multiple and intrinsically linked to enabling progress, as well as measuring it. Having this sense of 'education as a continuum' is one way in which you might think about the 'bigger picture' of assessment and further develop your own philosophy of it as your career develops.

Thinking in this 'bigger picture' way, it may be worth considering a cross-phase and/or a cross-curricular approach to assessment and your conception of what constitutes 'progress'. For example, if you were to think about pupils' progress in writing across *all* of their subjects, what kind of assessment outcomes might need to be analysed? And how might this necessitate a more holistic, cross-curricular approach to enabling pupils' learning? Alternatively, how might you think about an approach to teaching a given skill or content area if you were to consider what this looks like at both ends of the continuum: if you know where pupils have come from and could be going to, how might this enable you to challenge all pupils to progress to a higher degree of learning? There are potential links here to the ideas of Carol Dweck's 'growth mindset' theory: learners can only fully develop when they feel that there are no limitations on their potential learning. In practice, this might involve looking at an individual's progress in relation to themselves, rather than compared with their peers, and within the context of the skills, knowledge and behaviours upon which they have been working. Though this may seem several steps away from pupils' participation in more formalised, quantifiable assessments, this could be the key to their success in these assessments and beyond.

What if it's not on a spreadsheet?

The reality of working in education is that you will need to be able to produce and analyse data as a result of the assessments of your pupils' learning. Thinking back to the ideas of Chapter 4, where you thought about what you understand by 'progress' and 'over time', it could be an extension of your thinking in relation to the reflective task questions in that chapter to really delve into a further question about data production, analysis and tracking.

There are two key ways in which you could take your thinking about 'non-spreadsheetable' assessments further.

1. What opportunities might there be for creating other modes of 'capture'?

2. If it's not a on spreadsheet, does it matter? And does it matter in terms of both the value of other kinds of progress (Alexander, Black and Wiliam would argue that it does) and also in terms of whether or not it matters that all progress is somehow 'captured'?

These are potential questions to consider, even though you may not reach a conclusion, as part of developing your thinking and your expertise.

The first of these two questions suggests a range of potential approaches and opportunities. When thinking in this way, you are thinking about 'assessment for learning' and 'assessment for planning' as well as 'assessment of learning'. A range of modes of capturing assessment data and/or evidence of progress outside of spreadsheet (ie quantitative) data could include:

» giving written and/or oral feedback to pupils and then analysing their resultant response to this feedback (eg pupils revisit an answer given based on your written feedback, addressing the comments made);

» annotating lesson plans with examples of pupils' progress/achievements/ outcomes (eg noting each time a particular pupil puts up their hand to contribute in a whole-class context and tracking this over a series of lessons as part of looking at their developing confidence) and tracking this over time;

» links with self and peer-assessment opportunities, with pupils monitoring their own progress (this could be skills, knowledge, confidence, enjoyment, etc) over time;

» colleagues' observations of your lessons, focusing on specific progress markers (such as the confidence example above).

The second of these questions presents a more ideological opportunity for thought. There are many ways in which we as teachers think about the development of our pupils: to what extent all of this thought-processing can, could or should be captured is debatable. There is, of course, a point at which the burden of capturing everything that could be construed as indicative of progress becomes prohibitively cumbersome. There is also an extent to which the speed, implicitness and depth to which you are able to do this will increase as you gain experience and expertise as a classroom practitioner. Indeed, the work of Alexander, Black and Wiliam (to name but a few) would suggest that it is the overall impact that is important rather than capturing it – but that both the teacher and the learner should be able to see how progress has been enabled and where the learner has both been 'successful' and where they need to develop further. It is this latter point for which the analysis of data and evidence, be it on a spreadsheet or a remembered instance in a lesson, is a key part of planning the next steps of support, challenge and learning.

What is all of this data for anyway? How can I get 'behind' the data?

Whether on a spreadsheet, a sticky note or in your head, it is pointless to collect data unless you are going to make use of it. We've discussed the various auditors of the quantitative data that is the mainstay of educational assessment evidence (the government, school leadership teams, inspectorate bodies, etc). However, you have the 'frontline' opportunity to make dynamic, everyday use of all kinds of assessment data to maximise the impact of your teaching on your learners.

Knowing your pupils – as individuals and as groups – is the 'trump card' for looking at assessment. This in-depth knowledge of the learners in your care will underpin your analysis of assessment data, your feedback to pupils and the ways in which you 'plan for progress' for them. This knowledge may come in part from the data that you both receive and contribute to about them: identified needs, membership of identified groups (FSM, Pupil Premium, etc), attendance, prior and projected attainment, test scores and assignment marks are all part of this picture of the learner. What this looks like in the classroom on a daily basis, the impact it has on an individual child's behaviours and how you might best support and challenge that individual is what the resultant analysis and experience of working with that child should yield. It is this latter kind of 'planning for progress' and 'assessment' which might sit at the heart of leveraging success for all learners.

It might also be useful to consider the potential relationship between assessment and reflection here. The potential for exploiting this as part of working with a reflective methodology (either an established one or that of your own construction) will be explored in Chapter 6, 'Pupils as Mirrors'.

So what? ◀ ◀ ◀

What difference will it make?

Developing high-quality, developmental approaches to assessing your pupils in a range of ways is very much the practical application of the 'big ideas' thinking above. By their nature, these ideas fall largely into the 'assessment for learning' and 'formative assessment' camps (see Chapter 1). However, you might also want to consider the potential for 'summative assessment' to be developmental. For this to be fully realised, you may need to think about the ways in which you could support your pupils to see such assessments as 'markers' in time, rather than the sole representation of their achievement at any given stage in their educational careers. For example, Year 11 (16 year-olds) students in England are often encouraged to see their GCSEs (or equivalent end of secondary school tests) as the most important tests that they will ever take: this is the same tune we sing at the end of Key Stage 5/to post-16 students about their A levels/equivalents, and the refrain repeats at the end of university courses, or as part of tests for those who enter employment and undertake tests/other forms of assessment as part of this. It may be that you consider how formalised assessments might be seen both as being important and worth the effort of working for but that they are both 'gateways' to another potential stage and, in many ways, assessing pupils' ability to do the assessment more than assessing their knowledge, skills or understanding per se.

These are important ideas but perhaps need a tangible, practical starting point in your practice. In thinking about how you might develop the depth and breadth of your collection and use of assessment evidence, you could consider:

>> ways of capturing qualitative evidence and data;

>> self- and peer-assessment opportunities and their potential impact on learners;

>> written and oral feedback and its developmental purposes;

>> links to 'modelling';

>> links to formative assessment principles;

>> links to reflection (see Chapter 6 – 'Pupils as Mirrors' for more detail on this particular aspect).

In a number of ways, these guiding questions build on the ideas, reflective task and practices explored in Chapter 3. They could also be used as a way of thinking about the 'big picture' which contextualises the everyday ways in which you work on the 'what', 'how', 'why' and 'effects' of assessment, which you can consider through Chapter 3, if you decide to think in depth about this aspect of your approaches to assessment first.

Reflective task ◀◀◀

Apply the big idea to a practical situation in the classroom

Think about the 'big picture' of the assessment data that you collect and use this framework to support this (the following example should support the depth and breadth of your thinking). This thinking should lead you into the practical tasks which follow in this chapter.

You could start by focusing on one group/class or you could look at one type of assessment data (eg end-of-term assessments) and look at that across a range of classes (if you teach 11–16 and/or post-16/secondary/FE) or a specific subject within the curriculum (if you teach early years/primary).

What is it?	How do you/could you collect this? Where does it come from?	Who are you collecting this for? What happens to this data/evidence?	How does this inform your teaching?	What impact could this have on learners and their progress? (positive/negative)	How could you make better use of this assessment evidence?
End-of-term/topic assessment marks					
In-lesson tasks (eg written piece, drawing, presentation, experiment, etc – specify what you're focusing on)					

In-lesson learning behaviours: • contribution to whole-class contexts; • enjoyment of learning; • peer–peer interactions; • listening skills.					
Other identified learning behaviours [qualitative data] (For you to complete)					
(For you to complete)					

Example   Using the tool

What is it?	How do you collect this? Where does it come from?	Who are you collecting this for? What happens to this data/ evidence?	How does this inform your teaching?	What impact could this have on learners and their progress? (positive/ negative)	How could you make better use of this assessment evidence?
End-of-term assessment marks	From marking of end-of-term work/ tasks: added into master year-group spreadsheet on in-school network.	For SLT monitoring; reporting to parents; as part of my own review of end-of-learning topic/scheme of learning. SLT analyse it as part of whole-school data and progress tracking. Parents receive a copy of the data as part of their child's report at the end of the academic year.	Highlights key areas of strength and development across the cohort. Use this to inform planning for following year (if end-of-year data) – teaching same content again, so may need revisions to planning. Can see which topics were most successful with particular groups of pupils – need to look at why this is and whether there were opportunities to address this during the lessons.	*Possible positives* Pupils who feel that they've done well are likely to be motivated to continue and feel validated in their work. Can look at trends over time and look at comparison between my group and the rest of the cohort – could be useful for group interventions and future planning. *Possible negatives* Pupils who feel that they haven't done well could be discouraged from working/ engaging – could contribute to idea of 'fixed mindset' for them re. their own achievement. More useful for planning for new groups/cohorts – has limited impact for my current group.	Possibly need to plan interim opportunities to feed back to pupils to support them to make more progress pre-assessment? Could use it to identify pupils whose work I want to use as 'model' responses in teaching for the next cohort. Could also use this evidence to inform differentiation (stretch and challenge) for the next round of teaching – need to look at how to mitigate challenges faced by underperforming groups/skill areas. Need to think about how to use AfL to look at interventions *before* summative assessments to mitigate limitations of usefulness for current group and maximise their progress pre-assessment.

Now what? ◀◀◀

Practical ways to implement this in the classroom

Having reviewed the 'big picture', this is an opportunity to think further about the implications of these ideas for your practice and your pupils' learning.

Practical task for tomorrow ◀◀◀

The intention of this task is to give you a starting point for the further tasks below and to look at how you might use reflection as a way of using 'assessment for planning' (as discussed in Chapter 1).

- Look at your lessons for tomorrow.

- For your plan for each of these lessons, highlight/annotate the following:

  - Where there are explicit assessments taking place (ie quiz as a plenary, peer feedback).

  - Where there are implicit assessments taking place (ie pupils sharing ideas with a partner and deciding which idea to share with the whole class, question and answer sequences).

  - Who's doing the assessing – you, pupils of themselves, pupils of their peers?

  - What the result of the assessment is intended to be.

- At the end of the day, look back at your annotations and think about these lessons now that you've taught them.

  - How effective were the approaches that you chose?

  - What are your tendencies in your planning – is there a 'go to' that you use as an approach to in-lesson assessment?

  - How might you develop the assessment opportunities in these lessons to a) provide more opportunities for developmental feedback for pupils; b) provide more opportunities for pupils to act on this feedback; c) create opportunities for pupil-led assessment?

- What might the impact of the above look like in terms of *specific* progress/ learning for pupils? What qualitative data might you note and analyse from this?

Practical task for next week ◀◀◀

Take your findings from the practical task above and:

- Observe at least one colleague, focusing on the same questions as those asked of your lessons.

- Take your observations from this and your learning from the practical task above:

  - Identify three strategies to use in your own teaching this week – one which focuses on pupils assessing themselves/their peers, one which enables pupils to act on the feedback that they receive, one which contributes directly to a summative assessment/preparation for this.

  - Plan for these to be included across your lessons for the week. Remember, it is the *strategy* you are replicating over the week, rather than the specific task/assessment activity: how many ways might you use the *strategy/its principles* over the course of the week? Why might this be a useful way of thinking about 'assessment' and its impact on your pupils?

  - Identify key, qualitative examples of progress/learning: which strategies enable what kind of progress tracking? How might this provide you with some key ideas to take forward?

Practical task for the long term ◀◀◀

In your planning, use the following model/key questions to plan for assessment (summative and formative) – to plan for pupils' progress, learning and achievement.

Here, the following understanding of the levels of planning is assumed:

- short-term planning – individual-lesson level (daily and/or weekly);

- medium-term planning – a scheme/unit of work or a sequence of lessons over a period of time (ie a topic, half-term, term, etc);

- long-term planning – over a sustained period, such as the academic year, syllabus delivery time (eg the duration of the GCSE course).

Short-term planning
• How does this link to the previous lesson?
• How does this link to the next lesson?
• Links to learning (skills, knowledge, behaviours) in other subjects?
• Links to medium-term summative assessment(s) outcomes/activities?
• What gaps in experience might this assessment show?
• How can I support pupils to bridge gaps?
• How might assessment help this? What strategies/assessment activities could I use: why?
• What qualitative impact do I intend to have on pupils?
• What quantitative impact do I intend to have on pupils?
• How will I know this? How will I monitor/capture this?
• Why is this important?
• Implications for medium-term planning?

Medium-term planning
• How does this link to the previous medium-term plan?
• How does this link to the next medium-term plan?
• Links to learning (skills, knowledge, behaviours) in other subjects?
• Links to long-term assessment(s) outcomes/activities?
• What gaps in experience might this assessment show?
• How can I support pupils to bridge gaps?

- How might assessment help this? What strategies/assessment activities could I use: why?

- What qualitative impact do I intend to have on pupils?

- What quantitative impact do I intend to have on pupils?

- How will I know this? How will I monitor/capture this?

- Why is this important?

- Implications for long-term planning?

Long-term planning

- How does this link to the previous academic year?

- How does this link to the previous key stage in learning?

- How does this link to the next academic year?

- How does this link to the next key stage in learning?

- Links to learning (skills, knowledge, behaviours) in other subjects?

- What gaps in experience might this assessment show?

- How can I support pupils to bridge gaps?

- How might assessment help this? What strategies/assessment activities could I use: why?

- What qualitative impact do I intend to have on pupils?

- What quantitative impact do I intend to have on pupils?

- How will I know this? How will I monitor/capture this?

- Why is this important?

- Implications for future planning and/or pupils' transition to the next academic year?

What next? ◀◀◀

Further reading

Council for the Curriculum, Examinations and Assessment (CCEA) (nd) Cross-Phase Transitions. [online] Available at: http://ccea.org.uk/curriculum/assess_progress/ assessment_practice/cross_phase_transitions (accessed 16 June 2019).

Fletcher-Wood, H (2018) *Responsive Teaching*. Oxford: Routledge.

Ofsted (2018) *School Inspection Handbook*. Manchester: Ofsted.

References

Alexander, R (2004) *Towards Dialogic Teaching: Rethinking Classroom Talk*. Cambridge: Dialogos.

Black, P and Wiliam, D (1998) *Inside the Black Box: Raising Standards Through Classroom Assessment*. London: King's College School of Education.

Dweck, C (2008) *Mindset: The New Psychology of Success*. New York: Ballantine Books.

Chapter 6   Pupils as mirrors

What? (The big idea)

Pupils' 'progress over time' as a potential starting point for reflective practice

This chapter will explore and highlight the ways in which pupils' progress might be demonstrative of the quality of teaching and learning, linking with the ideas in Chapters 4 and 5. In this chapter, we will look at the ways in which you might use evidence/data from your impact on pupils to support assessments of and reflections on your own practice, with this being a way of thinking holistically about 'professional practice' in a pupil-focused manner.

Assessing our learners as part of assessing ourselves

In previous chapters, there has been discussion of what might be understood by 'pupil progress over time': in these chapters, the importance of a range of evidence from and of pupils' learning has been highlighted as key to thinking meaningfully about what learning can look like and how we perceive progress.

Throughout your career, there are ways in which your work as a teacher might be 'assessed' through pupil progress evidence. Whether in the evidence that you presented as part of your assessment for Qualified Teacher Status, or in a presentation of pupils' performances to school governors as an established in-school leader, or in your lesson-by-lesson planning in your everyday practice, pupils' learning can be seen to be at the heart of your work as a teacher.

Framing your professional reflections as a teacher

Some potential ways of 'getting behind the data' were explored in Chapter 5. As well as considering a range of qualitative and quantitative data, using knowledge of learners (as individuals and as groups) and really focusing on actual impact on pupils, you could also consider the approaches that you are taking to your reflection.

It is likely that, explicitly or not, your initial experiences of being a teacher have included some form of 'reflective methodology': a structured or framed approach to interrogating your practice which moves beyond 'what went well' and 'even better if'. The ideas of Brookfield and Tripp, who both published education-specific reflective models, might seem to align with a learning evidence-centred approach to thinking about the impact of teaching.

Brookfield (1995) suggested that teachers reflect on their practice using four lenses:

1. the 'autobiographical' – self-reflection;

2. the students' eyes – feedback from pupils;

3. our colleagues' experiences – peer-assessment (feedback, discussion, collaborative planning);

4. theoretical literature – scholarly reading, theory, pedagogy.

The second viewpoint, pupils, might in the context of 'assessment' be what evidence, data and specific examples of pupils' learning say about the quality and impact of a teacher's practice. The key to leveraging the potential of Brookfield's approach is to use all four viewpoints, combining them to 'assess' your practice in your reflection.

Tripp (1993) posits the idea that being a teacher requires developing a professional approach that comes through the exercising of critical analysis. To do this, Tripp outlines a process through which the teacher deduces the moments which are key to identifying patterns and routines in their practice which have an impact (positively or negatively). Even where a moment may seem mundane, it is the analytical, reflective process which illuminates those which might be deemed 'critical'.

The reflective and practical tasks which follow in this chapter suggest some ways in which you might 'assess' your own practice using a combination of reflective methodology and evidence from pupils' learning. Whether one of Brookfield's lenses (1995) or Tripp's incidents (1993), you can hold up pupils' learning as a mirror to reflect on your practice here.

So what? ◀ ◀ ◀

What difference will it make?

The reflective task here is a revised version of the reflective tasks in Chapters 1 and 3: it is intended to take your thinking from that point further (though it will also be useful if you're looking at this chapter first) as well as preparing you for the practical tasks in the 'Now What?' section that follows. This task is also based on Brookfield's 'lenses' (1995).

The key aim of this task is to explore how you might use assessment as part of your development as a reflective practitioner. Over time, and through the work that you'll do as part of this and other chapters in this book, you could use these 'framing' questions as a starting point for your on-going development of your professional understanding and practical use of assessment.

There are three broad questions underpinning this task.

1. What might link your ideas about and approaches to assessment and your approach to reflecting on your practice?

2. How does this influence the ways in which you and pupils use the findings from assessment in your classroom?

3. How might you use this to develop your practice further to best impact upon pupils' learning?

Reflective task ◀◀◀

Apply the big idea to a practical situation in the classroom

Lens 1 – autobiographical lens	Lens 2 – learners' eyes
What have you observed?	What have you observed/have learners' demonstrated to you?
How do you know what you know (specific examples)?	How do you know what you know (specific examples)?
What have you learned? Why?	What have you learned? Why?
How might this influence your practice in the future? Why?	How might this influence your practice in the future? Why?
Intended impact on your learners? Why?	Intended impact on your learners? Why?

Assessment for reflection: examining impact of planned interventions for ONE pupil in your lessons over the past six lessons ('progress over time'). *You can adapt this as needed to extend/more tightly focus your reflection.*

• What might link your ideas about and approaches to assessment and your approach to reflecting on your practice?

• How does this influence the ways in which you and your pupils use the findings from assessment in your classroom?

• How might you use this to develop your practice further to best impact upon pupils' learning?

Lens 3 – colleagues' eyes	Lens 4 – literature
What have they observed/has their practice done to influence you (could be lesson observations, mentor meetings, planning discussions)?	What have you read?
How do you know what you know (specific examples)?	How do you know what you know (specific examples)?
What have you learned? Why?	What have you learned? Why?
How might this influence your practice in the future? Why?	How might this influence your practice in the future? Why?
Intended impact on your learners? Why?	Intended impact on your learners? Why?

Example   Using the tool

Early years mathematics

This example focuses on one of the areas from the task above.

Lens 3 – colleagues' eyes
What have they observed/has their practice done to influence you (could be lesson observations, mentor meetings, planning discussions)?   • VO's lesson – as well as visual models of the quantities, the teacher used verbal models to link to work on sounds from early reading work. Built on prior learning to look at whether gaps were in understanding of the concept or the language.   • VO used children who could link number to the objects to demonstrate to those who couldn't – they used paired work to ascertain who could/couldn't do this.   How do you know what you know (specific examples)?   • Children could all work out which pile had more or less in it. BB and TW could not do this from just the numbers of things in the piles – language of the quantities was the barrier rather than being able to order them based on what they could see.

What have you learned? Why?

- *Pupil-generated models can both be used to teach the idea and to 'test' children's understanding of it. Demonstration of the knowledge/understanding is both application and assessment.*

- *Children were more confident in 'having a go' with the sorting of the piles, using numbers, etc when in pairs than in whole class – stakes were lower, they could 'rehearse' answers and if they made a mistake, it was just between them and their partner (but observed by the teacher).*

How might this influence your practice in the future? Why?

- *Plan for pupils to create some of the models in future lessons – use this as a way to test whether they've 'got it' or not – opportunity for them to both apply learning and for me to assess it.*

- *Think about how I could use children working in pairs/small groups instead of trying to check on their learning in whole-class moments – all children able to share, all children can be confident in 'having a go' as well as sharing what they've done/can do.*

Intended impact on your learners? Why?

- *Children rely on themselves/each other rather than me for models of 'how to do' what we're learning – part of making them Key Stage 1 'ready'.*

- *Children's confidence to try replaces 'getting it right' as the driver – can plan for more challenge – as they share processes of learning as well as outcomes.*

Now what?

Practical ways to implement this in the classroom

These tasks link back to the tasks and thinking that you did in Chapter 3, as well as to the reflective task in this chapter. They are designed to frame your application of reflection and reading from this chapter as well as linking to Tripp's 'critical incident analysis' model (1993).

These tasks do not require you to have first completed those from Chapter 3: they are intended to build on the practices there but also 'stand alone' to frame your thinking about the potential use of 'pupils' progress over time' as a way into reflecting on your practice.

Focus	One identified pupil in one lesson
Before teaching – assessment for planning	
'Big question'	**Supporting prompt questions**
Effects?	• What impact do you intend to have on the pupil?
What?	• What will *you* do to enable this learning to happen? Think about: questions; activities; praise; challenge; support. What else? • What will the *pupil* do to enable this learning to happen? Think about: questions; activities; praise; challenge; support. What else?
How?	• How will *you* do the things above? • How will the *pupil* do the things above? • How might you anticipate barriers to learning/ misconceptions/things which might hinder progress? • How might you mitigate these? • How might you plan for challenge as well as support?
Why?	• What do you intend to achieve by using these approaches in this lesson? • Why is this learning important? • How might the pupil explore 'the why' (links with understanding) in the lesson through this?
After teaching – assessment for reflection	
'Big question'	**Supporting prompt questions**
What and how?	• What were the *three* most impactful moments in the lesson for the identified pupil? How do you know this? • What were the moments which might have limited the potential extent of the identified pupil's learning? How do you know this?

	• What were the *three* most impactful moments in the lesson for the whole class/group? How do you know this? How does/doesn't this align with the moments you identified for the one pupil you were initially focused on?
Why?	• Why were *your* approaches successful/not as successful as you'd hoped?
	• Why was what the *pupil* did successful/not as successful as you'd hoped?
	• Was this learning important? Why might you refine your 'intention' for the next lesson based on this lesson?
	• How did the pupil explore 'the why' (links with understanding) in the lesson through this?
Effects?	• What impact did you have on the pupil?
	• What impact did you have on the whole group/class?
How do you know what you know?	• What did learning look like in the lesson?
	• How do you know that learning did/did not take place?
	• How do you know whether the approach was successful or not?
	• What specific evidence/data/examples from the identified pupil's learning do you have from using this approach in the lesson?
So what?	• What are the implications for your future practice, based on your reflections?
	• How could you implement these practices in the long term?
	• Why and how might this impact positively on the identified pupil's learning in the future?
	• How could you use the *principles* of the approach you used here but do things in a different way? Why?
	• How has this developed your professional skills, knowledge and understanding?

Practical task for next week ◀◀◀

Focus	Using the principles identified above to develop practice using assessment of pupil learning as a mode of evaluating impact

Before teaching – assessment for planning

'Big question'	Supporting prompt questions
Effects?	• What impact do you intend to have on pupils this week? What does this look like in terms of pupils' learning (be specific)?
What?	• What principles from the task above (from one lesson) are you going to use this week? • What will *you* do to enable this learning to happen? Think about: questions; activities; praise; challenge; support. What else? • What will *pupils* do to enable this learning to happen? Think about: questions; activities; praise; challenge; support. What else?
How?	• How will *you* do the things above? • How will *pupils* do the things above? • How might you anticipate barriers to learning/ misconceptions/things which might hinder progress? • How might you mitigate these? • How might you plan for challenge as well as support?
Why?	• What do you intend to achieve by using these approaches? • Why is this learning important? • How might pupils explore 'the why' (links with understanding) in the lesson through this?

'Big question'	Supporting prompt questions
What and how?	• What were the *three* most impactful approaches during the week? How do you know this? • What were the moments which might have limited the potential extent of the learning? How do you know this? • How could you: – identify the principles behind the approaches? – use these as a starting point for your future practice/thinking?
Why?	• Why were *your* approaches successful/not as successful as you'd hoped? • Why was what *pupils* did successful/not as successful as you'd hoped? • Why might you refine or build your 'intention' for the next week's teaching based on this week? • How did pupils explore 'the why' (links with understanding) during the week?
Effects?	• What impact did you actually have on pupils this week?
How do you know what you know?	• What did learning look like (key, specific examples)? • How do you know that learning did/did not take place (key, specific examples)? • How do you know whether the approaches were successful or not (key, specific examples)?
So what?	• What are the implications for your future practice, based on your reflections? • How could you implement these practices in the long term? These will be your 'principles for success'. • Why and how might this impact positively on learning in the future? • How has this developed your professional skills, knowledge and understanding?

Practical task for the long term ◄◄◄

Focus	Over a term's worth of teaching, use the 'principles for success' developed above and a focus on impact on pupils to: • evaluate the efficacy of your 'principles for success'; • identify 'principles for success' for future practice.

Before teaching – assessment for planning

'Big question'	Supporting prompt questions
Effects?	• What impact do you intend to have on pupils by using these principles?
What?	• What will *you* do to enable learning to happen by using these principles? Think about: questions; activities; praise; challenge; support. What else? • What will *pupils* do to enable learning to happen by using these principles? Think about: questions; activities; praise; challenge; support. What else?
How?	• How will *you* do the things above? • How will *pupils* do the things above? • How might you anticipate barriers to learning/misconceptions/things which might hinder progress? • How might you mitigate these? • How might you plan for challenge as well as support?
Why?	• Why will these principles enable pupils to realise the intended learning? • Why is this important? • How might pupils explore 'the why' (links with understanding) through this?

'Big question'	Supporting prompt questions
What and how?	• What were the *three* most impactful approaches over the term? How do you know this? • What were the approaches which might have limited the potential extent of the learning? How do you know this?
Why?	• Why were *your* approaches successful/not as successful as you'd hoped? • Why was what *pupils* did successful/not as successful as you'd hoped? • How did pupils explore 'the why' (links with understanding) over the term?
Effects and 'how do you know what you know'?	• What did the most successful learning look like this term (specific examples)? • How do you know that learning did/did not take place (specific examples)?
So what?	• What are the implications for your future practice, based on your reflections? • How could you implement these practices in the long term (over the next year)? • Why and how might this impact positively on pupils' learning and your practice in the future? • How has this process developed your professional skills, knowledge and understanding?

What next?

Further reading

Black, P and Wiliam, D (1998) *Inside the Black Box: Raising Standards Through Classroom Assessment*. London: King's College School of Education.

Kolb, D (1984) *Experiential Learning: Experience as the Source of Learning and Development*. Englewood Cliffs, NJ: Prentice-Hall.

References

Brookfield, S (1995) *Becoming a Critically Reflective Teacher*. San Francisco, CA: Jossey-Bass.

Tripp, D (1993) *Critical Incidents in Teaching: Developing Professional Judgement*. London: Routledge.

Chapter 7   Pupils are doing it for themselves

What? (The big idea)

Self- and peer-assessment for developing metacognition to enhance progress

Self- and peer-assessment can be seen as ways in which pupils might 'do' the kinds of assessment practices which Booth's 2017 article (see Chapter 1) identified. Booth (2017) sets these practices out as developmental learning opportunities: learning intentions; success criteria; eliciting (quality) evidence of pupil learning; feedback; peer- and self-assessment.

Mujis et al's (2019) analysis and subsequent recommendations in the Education Endowment Foundation's *Metacognition and Self-Regulated Learning: Guidance Report* outline the relationship between metacognition and the enablement of pupils' progress. Among the seven recommendations made in the report, the following might most closely align with the assessment practices identified by Booth (2017).

Explicitly teach pupils metacognitive strategies, including how to plan, monitor, and evaluate their learning.

» *Explicit instruction in cognitive and metacognitive strategies can improve pupils' learning.*

» *While concepts like planning, monitoring and evaluating can be introduced generically, the strategies are mostly applied in relation to specific content and tasks, and are therefore best taught this way.*

» *A series of steps – beginning with **activating prior knowledge** and leading to **independent practice** before ending in **structured reflection** – can be applied to different subjects, ages and contents.*

(Mujis et al, 2019, p 6)

Assessment is key to realising the three metacognitive concepts mentioned here. The practical explorations of assessment for learning, assessment for planning and assessment for reflection that have been framed in this book very much key into this idea. As much as teachers might use these 'assessment for...' practices, the same approaches could become pupil-delivered: pupils use the information, data, evidence and questions arising from them to plan, monitor and evaluate their own learning. By doing so, Mujis et al's findings would intimate that pupils' learning becomes more profound, long-lasting and meaningful.

But how can teachers draw together the principles of metacognition, assessment and reflective practice to enable *pupils* to be the drivers? The reflective and practical tasks which follow here provide a potential starting point for your thinking: indeed, they aim to scaffold your own metacognitive approach to your professional learning. You could consider how, ultimately, this could become the core model for supporting and challenging your pupils to truly drive their own 'assessment *for* learning'.

So what? ◀ ◀ ◀

What difference will it make?

This task adapts the model from the reflective task in Chapter 6 to focus on peer- and self-assessment approaches in your current and growing experience. Over time, and through the work that you'll do/have done as part of this and other chapters in this book, you could use these 'framing' questions as a starting point for your on-going development of your professional understanding and practical use of assessment.

There are three broad questions underpinning this task.

1. What might link your ideas about and approaches to self- and peer-assessment?

2. How does this influence the ways in which you and your pupils use the findings from these kinds of assessment in your classroom?

3. How might you use this to develop your practice further to best impact upon pupils' learning?

The questions which sit around these broad questions link to a reflective model based on Brookfield's (1995) 'four lenses'.

Reflective task ◀◀◀

Lens 1 – autobiographical lens	Lens 2 – learners' eyes
What have you observed?	What have you observed/have learners' demonstrated to you?
How do you know what you know (specific examples)?	How do you know what you know (specific examples)?
What have you learned? Why?	What have you learned? Why?
How might this influence your practice in the future? Why?	How might this influence your practice in the future? Why?
Intended impact on your learners? Why?	Intended impact on your learners? Why?

Assessment for reflection: examining the impact of self- and peer-assessment in six of your lessons over the past three weeks ('progress over time').
You can adapt this as needed to extend/more tightly focus your reflection.

- What might link your ideas about and approaches to peer- and self-assessment?

- How does this influence the ways in which you and pupils use the findings from these kinds of assessment in your classroom?

- How might you use this to develop your practice further to best impact upon pupils' learning?

Lens 3 - colleagues' eyes	Lens 4 - literature
What have they observed/has their practice done to influence you (could be lesson observations, mentor meetings, planning discussions)?	What have you read?
How do you know what you know (specific examples)?	How do you know what you know (specific examples)?
What have you learned? Why?	What have you learned? Why?
How might this influence your practice in the future? Why?	How might this influence your practice in the future? Why?
Intended impact on your learners? Why?	Intended impact on your learners? Why?

Example   Using the tool

Key Stage 2

This example focuses on one of the areas from the previous task.

Lens 1 - autobiographical lens

What have you observed?

- In lessons where I'm introducing new ideas – tend to end up with lots of teacher talk and checking on pupils' learning by using questions to whole class.

- In lessons where I'm confident in the content, I'm more confident to let pupils' ideas and responses drive where the lesson goes, rather than sticking to my plan.

- I tend to use same approaches to self- and peer-assessment again and again:

  - self-assessment – tick what you've done well (based on success criteria shared with the class), mark what would be 'even better if' for improvements;

  - peer-assessment – marking each other's work cf self-assessment approach OR find a good example from what your partner did to share.

How do you know what you know (specific examples)?

- PR's group on Tuesday commented 'Do we have to do this again? Can't you tell us?' when I set up the self-assessment task. This did show that pupils know the routine, though, so could embed a different/more approaches.

- Pupils' confidence in using success criteria demonstrates that they are used to reviewing their own learning and can apply criteria/processes to it. This has led to pupils gaining confidence and positive responses to their own successes – E7 is one of the weakest students and they were delighted to be able to 'tick off' that they could do the things on the list tailored for them (but need to get them beyond this!).

What have you learned? Why?

- Pupils don't have a clear understanding of why they're doing self-/peer-assessment – clear in pupils' comments and the (lack of) quality in their responses.

- Similarly, the potential impact of self-/peer-assessment isn't being seen in what my pupils can do – they've become focused on 'getting it done' rather than what they're learning from it and how it's developing what they can do.

- Because they're just ticking against criteria, it becomes about what they've done/not done rather than what they've learned, how they could improve and why it is/is not good quality.

How might this influence your practice in the future? Why?

- Pupils setting/asking the assessment questions for AfL in lessons? A way of them planning for their learning and its assessment, as well as being a way of checking (for me and them) what they've learned through the quality and type of questions. (Would need to do some work on 'good questions' to really make this work.

- Wider range of approaches – could I try something like peer teaching to check on learning? This could also link with pupils building their own 'knowledge for teaching'. Need to think about how I could scaffold this to ensure quality, too.

Intended impact on your learners? Why?

- Independence – links with EEF report re. this improving learning outcomes.

- Pupils value 'but what did you learn?' as a key assessment for and assessment of learning question, as well as 'but how did you do?'. This enables them to monitor and evaluate learning as part of the metacognitive process.

Now what? ◀◀◀

Practical ways to implement this in the classroom

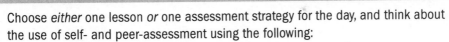

Practical task for tomorrow ◀◀◀

Choose *either* one lesson *or* one assessment strategy for the day, and think about the use of self- and peer-assessment using the following:

Who did it?	What was done?	How was it done?	Why do it like this?	Impact on learning? (How do you know what you know?)	How could you develop this in the future? (So what?)	
Teacher					As teacher-assessment	
					As peer-assessment	
					As self-assessment	
Pupils – peers					As peer-assessment	
					As self-assessment	
					As teacher-assessment	
Pupils – self					As self-assessment	
					As teacher-assessment	
					As peer-assessment	

What will I think about in the future as a result? (*So what?*)	*Next week:*	*This half-term:*	*This term:*

Practical task for next week ◀◀◀

Looking at your lessons for the week, consider the following:

Who did it?	What was done?	How was it done?	Why do it like this?	Impact on learning? (How do you know what you know?)	How could you develop this in the future? (So what?)	
Teacher					Reading	
					Observations of others	
					In my practice	
Pupils – peers					Reading	
					Observations of others	
					In my practice	
Pupils – self					Reading	
					Observations of others	
					In my practice	

What will I do to develop my practice in the future as a result? (So what?)	This half-term:	This term:	This year:

Practical task for the long term ◀◀◀

Every term, come back to the following questions: the idea here is that you are reviewing your 'big picture' knowledge, understanding and skills for 'assessment'. This is a way of framing and showing *your* 'progress over time'. These 'big questions' link back in particular to those posed in Chapters 1, 3 and 6, taking this thinking a few steps further.

What does it mean to me?
What influences my ideas about and approaches to assessment?

ASSESSMENT
- How do I know what I know? *Think about*: practices; reading; feedback; evidence/data from pupils' learning. What else?

- So what? *Think about*: implications for future practice; why this is/is not important for pupils' learning. What else?

- How does this influence the ways in which I and my pupils use assessment in my classroom?
- How does this look in my practice?

- What impact/effect does assessment have on the children that I teach?

Why is this important for supporting pupils' learning?
Why is it important for challenging pupils?
Why is this important for my professional development?

What next?

Further reading

Alexander, R (2004) *Towards Dialogic Teaching: Rethinking Classroom Talk*. Cambridge: Dialogos.

Assessment Reform Group (1999) *Assessment for Learning: Beyond the Black Box*. Cambridge: Cambridge School of Education.

Black, P and Wiliam, D (2006) *Assessment for Learning in the Classroom*. In Gardner, J (ed) *Assessment and Learning* (2nd ed) (pp 11–32). London: Sage.

Fletcher-Wood, H (2018) *Responsive Teaching*. Oxford: Routledge.

Spendlove, D (2009) *Putting Assessment for Learning into Practice*. London: Continuum.

Wiliam, D (2013) Assessment: The Bridge between Teaching and Learning. *Voices from the Middle*, 21(2): 15–20.

References

Booth, N (2017) What Is Formative Assessment, Why Hasn't It Worked in Schools, and How Can We Make It Better in the Classroom? *Impact – Journal of the Chartered College of Teaching*. [online] Available at: https://impact.chartered.college/article/booth-what-formativ e-assessment-make-better-classroom (accessed 16 June 2019).

Brookfield, S (1995) *Becoming a Critically Reflective Teacher*. San Francisco, CA: Jossey-Bass.

Mujis, D, Stringer, E and Quigley, A (2019) *Metacognition and Self-Regulated Learning: Guidance Report*. London: Education Endowment Foundation.

Acronym buster

Acronym	What does it stand for?	Notes/links
AfL	Assessment for Learning	
AoL	Assessment of Learning	
APP	Assessing Pupils' Progress	
BAME	Black, Asian and Minority Ethnic	
BfL	Behaviour for Learning	
BTEC	Business and Technology Education Council Awards	
CEDP	Career Entry Development Profile	
CPD	Continuing Professional Development	
DfE	Department for Education	
ECF	Early Career Framework	
ECT	Early Career Teacher	
EEF	Education Endowment Foundation	https://education endowmentfoundation.org. uk
FSM	Free School Meals	
(GCE) A level	General Certificate of Education Advanced Level	Also known as 'A2'
(GCE) AS level	General Certificate of Education Advanced Subsidiary Level	
GCSE	General Certificate of Secondary Education	
GNVQ	General National Vocational Qualification	
HEI	Higher Education Institute	
INSET	In-Service Training	
ITE	Initial Teacher Education	

Acronym	What does it stand for?	Notes/links
ITT	Initial Teacher Training	
KPI	Key Performance Indicator	
LAC	Looked-After Children	
MESH	Mapping Education Specialist knowHow	www.meshguides.org
NFER	National Foundation for Educational Research	
NQT	Newly Qualified Teacher	
NVQ	National Vocational Qualification	
Ofqual	Office of Qualifications and Examinations Regulation	
Ofsted	Office for Standards in Education, Children's Services and Skills	
pGCE	Professional Graduate Certificate of Education	
PGCE	Post-Graduate Certificate of Education	
PISA	Programme for International Student Assessment	
PRP	Performance-Related Pay	
QCDA	Qualifications and Curriculum Development Authority	
QTS	Qualified Teacher Status	
RQT	Recently Qualified Teacher	
SATs	Standard Attainment Tests	Based on the original name for these tests – now a colloquialism. SATs are also known as National Curriculum Assessments and end of key stage assessments.
SEND	Special Educational Needs and Disabilities	

Index